(continued)

Young Children Reinvent Arithmetic:
Implications of Piaget's Theory, 2nd Edition
CONSTANCE KAMII

Managing Quality in Young Children's Programs:
The Leader's Role
MARY L. CULKIN, ED.

Supervision in Early Childhood Education:
A Developmental Perspective, 2nd Edition
JOSEPH J. CARUSO & M. TEMPLE FAWCETT

The Early Childhood Curriculum:
A Review of Current Research, 3rd Edition
CAROL SEEFELDT, ED.

Leadership in Early Childhood:
The Pathway to Professionalism, 2nd Edition
JILLIAN RODD

Inside a Head Start Center:
Developing Policies from Practice
DEBORAH CEGLOWSKI

Windows on Learning:
Documenting Young Children's Work
JUDY HARRIS HELM, SALLEE BENEKE, &
KATHY STEINHEIMER

Bringing Reggio Emilia Home: An Innovative
Approach to Early Childhood Education
LOUISE BOYD CADWELL

Master Players: Learning from Children at Play
GRETCHEN REYNOLDS & ELIZABETH JONES

Understanding Young Children's Behavior:
A Guide for Early Childhood Professionals
JILLIAN RODD

Understanding Quantitative and Qualitative Research
in Early Childhood Education
WILLIAM L. GOODWIN & LAURA D. GOODWIN

Diversity in the Classroom: New Approaches to the
Education of Young Children, 2nd Edition
FRANCES E. KENDALL

Developmentally Appropriate Practice in "Real Life"
CAROL ANNE WIEN

Experimenting with the World:
John Dewey and the Early Childhood Classroom
HARRIET K. CUFFARO

Quality in Family Child Care and Relative Care
SUSAN KONTOS, CAROLLEE HOWES,
MARYBETH SHINN, & ELLEN GALINSKY

Using the Supportive Play Model: Individualized
Intervention in Early Childhood Practice
MARGARET K. SHERIDAN, GILBERT M. FOLEY,
& SARA H. RADLINSKI

The Full-Day Kindergarten:
A Dynamic Themes Curriculum, 2nd Edition

DORIS PRONIN FROMBERG

Assessment Methods for Infants and Toddlers:
Transdisciplinary Team Approaches
DORIS BERGEN

Young Children Continue to Reinvent Arithmetic—
3rd Grade: Implications of Piaget's Theory
CONSTANCE KAMII WITH SALLY JONES LIVINGSTON

Moral Classrooms, Moral Children: Creating a
Constructivist Atmosphere in Early Education
RHETA DEVRIES & BETTY ZAN

Diversity and Developmentally Appropriate Practices
BRUCE L. MALLORY & REBECCA S. NEW, EDS.

Changing Teaching, Changing Schools:
Bringing Early Childhood Practice into Public
Education–Case Studies from the Kindergarten
FRANCES O'CONNELL RUST

Physical Knowledge in Preschool Education:
Implications of Piaget's Theory
CONSTANCE KAMII & RHETA DEVRIES

Ways of Assessing Children and Curriculum:
Stories of Early Childhood Practice
CELIA GENISHI, ED.

The Play's the Thing: Teachers' Roles in Children's Play
ELIZABETH JONES & GRETCHEN REYNOLDS

Scenes from Day Care
ELIZABETH BALLIETT PLATT

Making Friends in School:
Promoting Peer Relationships in Early Childhood
PATRICIA G. RAMSEY

The Whole Language Kindergarten
SHIRLEY RAINES & ROBERT CANADY

Multiple Worlds of Child Writers:
Friends Learning to Write
ANNE HAAS DYSON

The Good Preschool Teacher
WILLIAM AYERS

The Piaget Handbook for Teachers and Parents
ROSEMARY PETERSON & VICTORIA FELTON-COLLINS

Visions of Childhood
JOHN CLEVERLEY & D. C. PHILLIPS

Starting School
NANCY BALABAN

Ideas Influencing Early Childhood Education
EVELYN WEBER

The Joy of Movement in Early Childhood
SANDRA R. CURTIS

POSSIBLE SCHOOLS

The Reggio Approach to Urban Education

ANN LEWIN-BENHAM

Foreword by Howard Gardner

Teachers College, Columbia University
New York and London

Published by Teachers College Press, 1234 Amsterdam Avenue, New York, NY 10027

Library of Congress Cataloging-in-Publication Data

Lewin-Benham, Ann.
    Possible schools : the Reggio approach to urban education / Ann Lewin-Benham ; foreword by Howard Gardner.
    p. cm.—(Early childhood education series)
    Includes bibliographical references and index.
    ISBN 0-8077-4652-5 (cloth)—ISBN 0-8077-4651-7 (pbk.)
    1. City children—Education (Early childhood)—United States. 2. Children with social disabilities—Education (Early childhood)—United States. 3. Early childhood education—Italy—Reggio Emilia. I. Title. II. Early childhood education series (Teachers College Press)
LC5131.L46 2006
372.21'09173'2—dc22   2005050579

ISBN 13:   ISBN 10:
0-978-0-8077-4651-6   0-8077-4651-7 (paper)
0-978-0-8077-4652-3   0-8077-4652-5 (cloth)

Printed on acid-free paper

Manufactured in the United States of America

13 12 11 10 09 08 07 06   8 7 6 5 4 3 2 1

In memory of my beloved mother
Florence Regina Levy White
1906–1998
Her watchword was joy.

Contents

Foreword

Generally, when in the mood for an engrossing tale, we look to fiction. It is the rare book of nonfiction that presents a compelling story. At first glance Ann Lewin-Benham's *Possible Schools* appears to chronicle the growth of a single remarkable school against the odds: the narrative features a sad ending, the closing of the school. As I read this book, however, I discern three stories, and they are ultimately hopeful ones.

The First Story: The Rise and Fall of the Model Early Learning Center. First, there is the story that Ann explicitly tells. A social entrepreneur to her bones, Ann launched no fewer than five schools, as well as a major children's museum in the nation's capital. By the late 1980s, she was ready for her biggest challenge: starting a model preschool—a Model Early Learning Center (MELC)—within the walls of the Capital Children's Museum. The preschool was designed specifically to serve the impoverished African American families in the neighborhood of the museum. The MELC was to be an existence proof: These youngsters could be as well served as the children of the members of the Museum's board—a board, incidentally, that kept lobbying Ann to move the museum that she had founded to the affluent suburbs.

The saga of the MELC has all the drama of a Hollywood movie. Can a well-meaning middle-class museum staff create and manage an educational establishment for a population that is poor, often alienated, lacking the social and financial capital that its staff take for granted? Why did the MELC run through five directors in the first few years of its operation? What happens when the museum's director, hopelessly overworked to begin with, takes the helm at the MELC? How do director, staff, and family react when a middle-aged woman with a thick Italian accent moves into the school and points out all of the things that are wrong? How do "progressive educational" ideas take soil with a population that holds traditional views of education? What, against overwhelming odds, enables the school to become an exemplary institution within a few years? How can the MELC survive in a climate of accountability, test scores, and the meltdown of the political and financial support in the District? And, tragically, why does the school close down 2 years after it achieves the highest form of accreditation?

By now, I hope that you have already raced to the text itself, if not taken an option on the movie rights. But for those of you who insist on reading a foreword through to its completion, let me mention the two other stories that are related within these pages.

The Second Story: The Remarkable Schools of Reggio Emilia. In the early 1960s, Loris Malaguzzi, a gifted and creative Italian educator, undertook a bold experiment in early childhood education. He determined to build an educational approach that mobilized the incredible energies and talents of young children and that foregrounded unprecedented cooperation among teachers, families, and the leaders of the community. Now, 40 years later, the infant-toddler centers and the preschools of Reggio Emilia are routinely cited as the most outstanding schools for young children in the world. Ann learned about these schools in the middle 1980s and began to visit them on a regular basis in the early 1990s. Like many of us who believed that we were knowledgeable about children and about preschool education, Ann was overwhelmed by what she saw with her own eyes throughout Reggio Emilia. She determined to re-create the salient aspects of the Reggio approach at the MELC. And when she discovered that this enterprise was far more complex than she had envisioned, she engaged Amelia Gambetti, the aforementioned Reggio educator, to spend a year at the MELC. How the Reggio approach becomes integrated into the DNA of the MELC constitutes the second dramatic thread of this book.

The Third Story: Progressive Ideas in Hostile Times. Ever since the time of John Dewey, a hardy band of educators scattered throughout the world has sought to construct educational endeavors that are termed "progressive." These demonstrations respect the minds and honor the worlds of children; and they seek to foster the most integral ties between the developing child and the community in which he or she now lives and may reside—and raise children—in the future.

Progressive education has never had an easy time. It goes against a long-standing prototype of what education should be: a process of taming and training, where adults with knowledge and power seek to mold young persons so that they will be prepared to carry out the tasks of the society, as currently constituted. It requires educators who have been well trained, who have faith in themselves and in their charges, who do a tremendous amount of preparation beforehand just so they can be flexible as the inherently unpredictable minutes and hours of school unfold. Even so, there are periods within American—and perhaps world—history when progressive educational ideas have been given some slack: I would mention the 1920s, the 1960s, and the early 1990s. The Model Early Learning Center was launched during such a period; but by the time the center had begun truly to absorb the principal ideas and practices of the Reggio model, a far more hostile climate with respect to educational innovation had swept the nation—one that endures as of this writing. Ultimately, the MELC was unable to survive in this forbidding milieu.

By now, I suspect that the pull toward a trio of complementary and overlapping narratives has become virtually irresistible. I want only to add that Ann Lewin-Benham is one of the most remarkable builders of educational institutions of our time; that she has kept incredibly detailed and helpful notes about the development of the MELC; that she is able to contextualize her accounts with apt connections to the psychological and educational literature as well as trenchant reflections of her own; and that she is a great storyteller. And I conclude with a reiteration that the stories told by her are hopeful ones. Reggio Emilia represents an existence proof that an entire community can build and maintain excellent schools. The Model Early Learning Center is an existence proof that schools in

the Reggio tradition can be created even in the most challenging urban disadvantaged areas. And the history of progressive ideas constitutes an existence proof
that the best ideas in education will endure. I join John Dewey, Loris Malaguzzi,
and Ann Lewin-Benham in the hope that they will ultimately prevail.

Howard Gardner
Cambridge, MA
February 2005

Introduction

Driven by concerns about young children's education, I founded the Model Early Learning Center (MELC) in 1988 to pursue my dream of a different kind of school. The school was born in chaos, but emerged as something cohesive in a handful of years. This book documents the story of the school's founding, its teachers, children, and families, and the relationships that developed among them.

The MELC occupied center stage when American interest in the preschools of Reggio Emilia, Italy, was first escalating. Anyone excited by these schools, hoping to provide quality early education, or concerned about young inner-city African American children will be intrigued by our struggles and inspired by our triumphs.

An era's accomplishments may lie forgotten until someone else rediscovers them. Today, when examples of good schools exist, why do we wait to replicate them? Babies are born every day, quickly growing into children who need good schools. Unfortunately, fallacious racial or social stereotypes constrain expectations for what some children can accomplish even though we know that each young child who is at risk because of poverty has the same potential as any other child. These facts—knowing what good schools look like and that stereotypes are constraining—have powerful implications for the business of education that shapes today's children, who in turn will shape our future.

The MELC's story is complex and layered, covering several years and including many voices. The players are its teachers, children, and families, as well as educators from the Reggio schools. Other factors are the museum environment where the school was located; the Washington, D.C. milieu; the mind-set of D.C. Public Schools, the MELC's contractor; the culture in which we live; the concerns of the school's families; and my beliefs as founder-director.

While the inspiration came from Italy, my perspective is rooted in American culture, the lens through which my opinions are filtered. Thus Reggio educators might not present the material as I interpret it. Moreover, understanding of complex phenomena, like the Reggio philosophy or a school's development, is never complete; the mind continues to ponder and new insights occur long after an experience ends. I shall always ask what we might have done differently.

In Chapter 1 I describe what influenced the MELC: its city's historical, political, social, and racial forces; its own neighborhood, institution, and families; my hopes; and the initial problems. In Chapter 2 I describe what I consider the essential characteristics of the Reggio Approach—the inspiration for what the MELC became—and portray the competence of those schools' children and teachers. Chapter 3 shows how the teachers and I first learned about Reggio, how we remade the MELC after our initial exposure, and the state of the school as we began our transition. Chapter 4 describes our first faltering steps as we attempted to put

Reggio ideas into practice. Chapters 5 and 6 relate Amelia Gambetti's advice, and Chapter 7 reveals the teachers' struggle as they began to change their practices with her as a collaborator. Chapter 8 conveys the families' concerns about literacy, how the MELC responded, and what Reggio practices and our culture brought to bear on the issue. Chapter 9 displays the teachers' increasing skill as, gradually, they learned to use essential Reggio practices such as the strategic use of materials, the art of documentation, and complex and challenging projects. Chapter 10 describes how families became involved, how other educators reacted, and how we changed as a result of our efforts. Chapter 11 explains why the MELC closed.

The specific information and many direct quotes in this book are based on extensive notes I took during meetings and lectures and while visiting in Reggio classrooms, in the MELC, and in other schools. All children's names have been changed and the individuals I have quoted by name have read and approved my reporting of their comments or perspective.

This book is for those who want to consider a different vision for early education. It is always a heroic effort to make a better school possible. It takes only a few parents, a handful of dedicated teachers, or an inspired principal to make changes locally, and each locale needs such heroes. I hope that this book will inform and excite passion for change, a change aptly described by George Leonard (1968): "Every child, every person can delight in learning. A new education is already here, thrusting up in spite of every barrier we have been able to build. Why not help it happen?" (p. 239).

For more than 25 years I struggled with ideas about what schools should be. My ideas began to coalesce after studying the work of many others, foremost among them Howard Gardner, Reuven Feuerstein, David Perkins, Mihaly Csikszentmihalyi, Lauren Resnick, Rochel Gelman, and cybernetics theorists. But only after working with the Reggio educators did I clarify my ideas about what schools *could* be. I am deeply indebted to Reggio founder Loris Malaguzzi, to Tiziana Filippini, Giovanni Piazza, Sandra Piccinini, Carlina Rinaldi, Sergio Spaggiari, and Vea Vecchi, to other remarkable Reggio educators as well, and especially to Amelia Gambetti, for the extraordinary vision evident in all their practices and the zealous dedication evident in each one's own work. I am equally indebted to MELC teachers Genet Astatke, Jennifer Azzariti, Wendy Baldwin, Deborah Barley, and Sonya Shoptaugh for their passionate belief in children and intrepid courage in daring to change; to the MELC children for their resilience and joy; to their families for trusting and collaborating with us. These educators, children, and families overcame every barrier to make a truly "model" early learning center.

Among the people who helped me with this book, foremost are my wise son Daniel Lewin, my caring husband Robert Benham, and my patient, perceptive editor Susan Liddicoat. Educators who offered encouragement are Jennifer Azzariti, Wendy Baldwin, Alexandra Cruickshank-Kretsinger, Amelia Gambetti, Howard Gardner, Jan Horne, Pamela Pierce, Sonya Shoptaugh, Maurice Sykes, Carol Anne Wein, and Marilyn Weinman. Marie Ellen Larcarda, Niko Pfund, and Lori Tate offered valuable advice.

Among the many people who helped me at The National Learning Center are Helen Parker, my assistant for 20 years; Sodartha Guion and Stephanie Giminez Mize, able administrators; Sharon Hemphill, Linda Putnam, Greg Gauthier, Stan Woodward, Bob Davis, Chris Lyman, Joyce Bonnett, James Blackman, Susan Albers,

Charles Gray, Bob Evans, Abdur Bey, Frenchie Jones, and Frank del Vecchio, all key staff members; Roy Mason and T Meyer, architects; Esthy Adler, Esther Coopersmith, Farol Seretean, and John Wilson, trustees. Each of these exceptional people and numerous others played their roles with brilliance time and again.

With gratitude I acknowledge the MELC teachers and Amelia Gambetti for many images. The floor plan was rendered with great care by archimania, Inc., Memphis, Tennessee. Certain translations from the Italian were provided with Leslie Morrow's or Lee Adair Lawrence's thoughtful assistance.

Today the MELC's story seems especially relevant for several reasons: Parents ask ill-prepared strangers to care for children at increasingly younger ages and for longer hours; politicians advocate test scores as the basis for funding education; and public school systems initiate programs for ever younger children. Because families' needs for child care and political and public demands are changing the early childhood landscape, the messages in this book are urgent for parents and policy makers as well as for educators. I hope the story of the MELC offers ideas and inspires others to undertake the enormous effort necessary to realize possible schools.

CHAPTER 1

Setting the Stage

Each educator has to consider society as one of his main targets for intervention.
Reuven Feuerstein, *don't accept me as I am*

From the start the Model Early Learning Center was influenced by the political and social climate of Washington, D.C. The city's aura and an isolated neighborhood provided the MELC's context. The start-up year, 1988, was dominated by the relationship with the Capital Children's Museum; the next 2 years were dominated by our inability to help the children become self-disciplined.

I had founded both the Capital Children's Museum and the Model Early Learning Center because I believed that schools were not effective, that educational experiences were far from equal, that even children best served were not sufficiently challenged. These beliefs and the concerns of the MELC's African American families shaped the school.

In this chapter I describe these factors—the political, social, historical, and personal forces—which determined what the school would become.

THE MELC'S CONTEXT

The peculiarities of the nation's capital impact all its residents. The city is unlike any other. The climate is palpably power-driven. There are racial and economic divides and politics dominates both. Neither city, county, nor state, Washington, D.C. has the responsibilities of all but the rights of none.

Political Peculiarities

In the 1990s, bumper stickers proclaimed: "D.C.—the last colony," a sign of antagonism between Congress's District Committee and some city residents. Washington was initially carved as a square from Maryland and Virginia, with the Potomac River in the middle. Most land west of the Potomac was later returned to Virginia, leaving a jagged cut, a metaphor for the national-local schism. Congress held Washington in a vise as a federal protectorate for the city's first two centuries. After the Civil War and Reconstruction, oversight of Washington fell increasingly to southern congressmen who controlled the District Committee. Power from the highest echelons reverberates in local affairs because individuals vie for political favor and organizations rely on federal funding. The MELC was no exception.

For 2 centuries Washingtonians had no political representation. Only in 1963 were they given the right to vote for the U.S. President, and in 1967, the authority to elect their school board. There was no elected mayor until 1973 when Congress finally replaced its own management with an elected city council and home rule. Washington still has no elected congressional representative and therefore no voice in Congress. Consequently, some residents feel disenfranchised; others thirst to be national players. Others, infected by the power-seeking milieu, fiercely covet any position with a title.

Without a voting representative, no one on Capitol Hill has chips to trade for Washington interests, a tough position with the city, its public schools, and many other local organizations all dependent on substantial congressional funding. Relationships between District officials and members of Congress range from cordial to tense, with congressional staff often as powerful as the elected members they serve. Many in the District government feel like puppets, their strings pulled by people whose interests lie elsewhere but who, nonetheless, cling to their power as the coin of the realm.

Social Anomalies

Substantial numbers of Washington-area residents leave every 2 to 6 years as members of Congress win or lose elections, administrations change, or military tours finish. The workforce is unique—lobbying groups, specialty law firms, think tanks, a health cadre, a huge media presence, over 4,500 not-for-profit organizations. A horde serves the federal government, many maintaining allegiance to hometowns and some officials returning home when appointments end. The poor are long-term residents, mainly invisible to higher socioeconomic groups except for media reports on inner-city crime or glitzy events on behalf of "in" charities serving the poor. Among the diverse economic strata, Washington had no Carnegie or Gates, industry titans who might ameliorate their city's poverty.

A TROUBLED NEIGHBORHOOD

In 1977, less than a decade after the assassination of Martin Luther King Jr., and as Jimmy Carter's presidency began, Rosalyn Carter toured Washington's blighted neighborhoods. "Do something about this," she commented on seeing the H Street Corridor where the MELC would be located. Although close to the grounds of the Capitol, H Street was a major divide between rich Capitol Hill and one of Washington's poorest neighborhoods. By the 1970s the press referred to the H Street Corridor as "slums in the shadow of the Capitol," an epithet triggering fear in many middle- and upper-class residents. Yet, H Street was where the Capital Children's Museum had become established and unused space in its ample facilities would house the MELC.

Recent History

Once thriving, the H Street Corridor's demise began in the 1940s, when its affluent Jewish population left for the suburbs. Middle-income African Americans, for whom the suburbs were "redlined," snapped up the homes. In the 1960s, a large enclave of substandard housing was razed in Southwest Washington. Displaced residents flooded the Corridor, the only affordable area near downtown. Townhouses were divided, with entire families renting one room. The middle-class African American population fled, businesses closed, crime festered. When H Street exploded in 1968 as one of Washington's three riot corridors following King's assassination, any remaining niceties vanished.

In 1978, just as the Capital Children's Museum moved onto H Street, a new overpass effectively made the Corridor a no-man's-land, an example of how so-called urban development can worsen the quality of life: "Laying a concrete slab on top of [the area], . . . buried [it] in shadow . . . its bustle and life forever gone. . . . Once friendly, now [the street] was frightening. . . . [no] caring neighbors, aware eyes" (Caro, 1974, pp. 521–523). This was H Street. From our building, cars backfiring were indistinguishable from gunshots. Block after bleak block housed pawnshops, bars, and liquor stores, along with a frequently untenanted grocery and a heavily barricaded drugstore. For decades storefronts remained boarded. No one from middle-class Washington or rich Capitol Hill would venture there.

Stabilization Effort

In 1978 the U.S. Department of Housing and Urban Development (HUD) granted $1.7 million to Capital Children's Museum (CCM) to purchase a full block on the Corridor's western end. HUD expected the museum to stabilize the area by spurring housing, attracting business, and dampening impressions of the Corridor as crime-ridden: The Museum was supposed to foment change. Within 5 years CCM had over 200,000 visitors annually. But the neighborhood remained isolated and H Street was still a barrier, despite the bustling Museum and real estate development to its south.

A SCHOOL IN A MUSEUM

The Model Early Learning Center (MELC) was one of several programs of The National Learning Center (TNLC), an entity that had evolved from the Capital Children's Museum in the early 1980s. When the MELC opened in 1989, TNLC included a junior high dropout-prevention school and teacher education programs. Well-established, both CCM and TNLC facilitated the preschool's start-up.

The Location Factor

At its inception in 1975, racial prejudice had almost destroyed the Capital Children's Museum. Located far from areas where its well-to-do board members felt safe, three quarters had resigned. The location remained a persistent issue. Nonetheless, CCM gained renown for innovative exhibits, which were covered by media worldwide. Visitors ranged from neighborhood children to national and international VIPs, none deterred by the location. The museum and the MELC shared a commitment. CCM's raison d'être became the MELC's: to offer children in poverty high-quality educational programs by locating in their midst.

While the location impinged on the museum, its impact on the children and families of the MELC was far more dire. Gunshots from the drug trade near the MELC children's homes were a constant source of stress. The MELC teachers were deeply concerned because 5-year-olds were used as lookouts during drug deals. Drug-related topics occurred regularly in the children's conversation. This mirrored the immediate neighborhood and the culture at large, which was permeated by drug-related messages—ads pitching drugs to consumers, children calmed down by drugs, the nefarious influences of gangs. Teachers read the obituaries daily, concerned whether anyone in the children's families had become victims of the drug trade. They tried to override the worst influences by making the school a haven.

The Museum Imprimatur

Surplus space on the fifth floor of the museum's massive building became the MELC's home. The school drew on the museum's reputation, design, and philosophy, and shared its spotlight as museum visitors—presidents' wives, foreign dignitaries, pop-culture stars—also visited the school. First Lady Barbara Bush officiated at the opening, cut the red ribbon, and read *Three Billy Goats Gruff* to the children.

The museum's preoccupation with design influenced the MELC's look: consistent, noncommercial graphics; quiet colors; uncluttered space; a clean aesthetic; explanatory texts. Both shared a Piagetian emphasis on learning through doing, a Vygotskian belief in the social nature of learning, and a Gardneresque commitment to the development of multiple intelligences.

The museum provided—as the MELC would also—an alternative to the negative images children receive through the media. The MELC teachers disliked the profusion of relationships on TV that range from rude to violent. Drama, humor, sports, cartoons—all depict people more likely to be mean than kind. Words like "I'm gonna hit you upside the head," whether spoken in jest or announcing imminent attack, are typical TV interactions. Even wild animal shows focus on attack and destroy, bringing fear into children's bedrooms. With TV viewing as a family pacifier, the teachers tried to help parents understand why children should be shielded from most TV shows. Museum exhibits provided alternatives; the MELC banned TV and made sure the school's program was gentle and humane.

THE FOUNDER'S PERSPECTIVE

The MELC evolved from my experiences as a parent and an educator. I was a Montessori teacher in the 1960s, and because I established new educational programs, was called a *change agent* in the 1970s. I was typical of those of my generation who, inspired by the writings of John Holt, Herbert Kohl, Jonathan Kozol, A. S. Neill, George Leonard, and other educator–social critics, hoped for a paradigm shift in education.

Background

I was especially committed to improving education for economically depressed children. This stemmed from my first job as a caseworker in a rural North

Carolina welfare department. I was responsible for 200 racially mixed clients, all poor. Since I had grown up privileged, this was my first exposure to poverty. I was overwhelmed by the burdens poverty imposes, by welfare rules that calculated payments on a meager basis, then paid only an arbitrary percentage, even less if clients grew collards or turnips. If they owned a jalopy or TV, they were ineligible. When I moved to Washington, I encountered an urban poverty far harsher. Most of my work attempted to redress poverty's burdens, for example, selecting CCM's neighborhood and insisting on remaining there. I hoped the MELC could demonstrate that its children, who met federal poverty guidelines for Head Start, were just as smart as rich children and the Reggio Approach just as right for them.

My son Danny's first school experience aroused my interest in education. In 1963 at 2 years old, he attended a play group for 2 hours twice a week. Moms were required to help. The toddlers ignored the cutting and pasting the teacher had prepared, ran about hectically, fought over toys, screamed incessantly, and spread food everywhere. The teacher was overwhelmed, the mothers passively disengaged or involved in a vain attempt to rein in the children. The structure was inadequate, the environment underprepared, the parents' role undefined. After 2 weeks we withdrew. The experience was a harbinger that finding schools for Danny would prove frustrating.

Over 3 decades I founded five schools, and in the mid-1970s, when I established the Capital Children's Museum, I naively hoped children's museums might supplant schools. In the 1980s as we expanded CCM into The National Learning Center, we opened schools and other educational programs, many targeting economically disadvantaged children.

Motivation

In the late 1980s my concerns culminated in the attempt to make a model early learning center. It seemed that schools confounded some children, bored others, and for the majority of students (and teachers, as well) failed to spark imagination or curiosity—two hallmarks of learning. I was especially concerned as dichotomies between rich and poor widened when new technologies exploded. Since the 1970s I had followed new research of critical importance to education: in neuroscience, on brain functioning; in cybernetics, on system functioning; in psychology, on human cognition and emotion; and in social science, on family systems and *social cognition*, that is, interaction with others in the learning process. Yet, except for a few attempts, only rarely did practices reflect new theories. And questions kept nagging: How can teachers excite children to learn? What should a good school look like?

My concerns about poverty and my interest in new theories coalesced in the MELC. If the new understandings could converge in practice, they could create profound changes in educating children. Strong schools could emerge from a new paradigm formulated on relationships—teacher and administrator, school and family, adults and children, child and group, people and environment, school and community—as catalysts for learning.

My role as the MELC's founder and executive director was to project a vision. I hired key staff and nurtured those with promise, raised funds, managed cash flow. I designed the MELC's environment and forged a relationship with Reggio leaders. Once Amelia Gambetti, our expert Reggio consultant, began her residency, she and the teachers did the visible work. Behind the scenes I ensured that the MELC had ample space, staff, materials, and funds. I collaborated with Reggio leaders to present two national symposia, other teacher education programs, and a museum exhibit. I began staff development programs for teachers in the D.C. Public Schools. I met the press and brought innovative thinkers from education and psychology into the school. Those were my roles in the MELC, as they had been in TNLC, all driven by my belief that there was a new vision for what a school could be.

A DIFFICULT BEGINNING

Starting the MELC was enormously difficult. Before the school opened, two major problems were solved by CCM administrator Sodartha Guion. Sodartha was a tall woman with an elegantly sculpted face. Some read her aura as severe. Had she been a principal before schools were unsettled by drugs and weapons, she could have handled any problems with mere stance and glance: When she drew herself up, shoulders squared, arms akimbo, and eyes glaring, no one dared cross her.

The first problem occurred with principals in the public elementary schools. The D.C. Public Schools had designated neighborhoods of the six elementary schools closest to us as those from which our students would come. Fearful their enrollment might decline, the principals refused to provide lists of potential enrollees. A former D.C. Public Schools employee, Sodartha had been a public school system administrator who made things happen. Now she used her IOU's in the "girlfriend" network to produce lists.

The second problem occurred when the head of a city regulatory agency refused to license the MELC if it occupied the fifth floor. Recently lambasted by media coverage for fires that had destroyed two home-based day care centers, the agency was intransigent: The MELC would *not* be licensed above ground floor. Two weeks later, Sodartha reported we could use the fifth floor. I imagine she simply stared down the agency's chief.

The MELC opened with its first twelve children on December 4, 1989. They ranged from 3 to 5 years old. We added more children gradually to reach our full complement of 36. We operated under a contract to the D.C. Public Schools, a structure like some of the charter schools that were beginning to emerge in the late 1980s. Our contract stipulated that the MELC's children would be from Head Start–eligible families, although we were not in any way a Head Start program. Within 4 months, it became evident that we could neither discipline the children effectively nor put new theories into practice.

The first two directors of the MELC faced incredible behavior problems: One child, emitting blood-chilling shrieks, constantly hurtled his prone body across the floor; another had at least three titanic tantrums daily; a third screamed almost incessantly; and a fourth punched, hit, or kicked continuously. One child would have been challenging; four were overwhelming. The first director resigned after 4 months, and so did the second.

The third director stabilized the school by defining staff responsibilities: Teachers were to teach; aides were to manage the classroom, which meant addressing unsettled behavior. The hurtling child was dismissed; the tantrum-throwing child was withdrawn by a parent; the other two, when firmly restrained, learned to control themselves. The school calmed because the director insisted that children and teachers alike adhere strictly to four rules that every preschool teacher knows: Use your walking feet; use your quiet voice; keep your hands to yourself; put your things away. When the director applied these rules rigorously—requiring that teachers not call across the room and insisting that no matter what the provocation, teachers remain calm and not rush—the children quieted down. Within 4 months the children gained enough self-discipline for concentrated, extended work to begin. But the program remained mundane, neither visionary nor innovative, although settled now, thanks to the Classroom Management Rules.

THE AFRICAN AMERICAN PERSPECTIVE

Schools are never isolated. They are inseparable from the culture of their time and place. In the 1980s, Washington was racially fractured. The MELC families were all in the 17.3% of Washington's population who live in poverty (U.S. Census, 2001)). Middle- and upper-income families living near the Capitol or in a narrow strip of northwest Washington could drive their children to private school, traverse the city's length, join its economic, cultural, political, or nightlife, and never see a poor neighborhood. The first Leadership Washington program in 1987 educated a cross-section of community leaders about education, jobs, justice, governance, and health. The session on race was met with awkward silence, lowered heads, tightened knuckles. In the 1980s, the subject of racial prejudice was taboo in racially mixed company.

Historical Factors

As waves of northward migration following the Civil War brought increasing numbers of African Americans to Washington, racial tensions grew. Some of the MELC's families were descendants of the migrations. This history cast its shadow over the school: Members of Congress authorized our funds, but our families were farthest from their interests. Moreover, the majority of African American Washingtonians were removed from the national scene, impacted by federal government poverty programs, yet absent from policy making or implementation.

In 1989, although the era of political correctness had barely begun, there was great sensitivity about words connoting race. We were not to refer to our children as *poor* or our location as *inner-city*. Words like *poverty*, *disadvantaged*, *disenfranchised*, *undereducated*, *at-risk*, and *urban* carried overtones. So, despite our determination to have a majority African American staff, we advertised without reference to race. But the staff's race did not concern our families.

Families' Concerns

Our families' concerns were lack of job opportunities, inadequate transportation, substandard housing, insufficient health care, and crime-ridden neighborhoods. Like all families, they wanted a safe neighborhood, steady work, good education for their children, and respect. While I wanted to show respect to our families by hiring an African American staff, they wanted their children to be educated, disciplined, loved, and respected. The teachers' belief in their dignity, not the teachers' race, was what mattered. In the MELC, awkwardness about race was a white not a black issue.

Families were accepting of the school from the first. The school was aesthetically pleasing; it had an abundance of materials from which children could choose their activities; and television was never used. The teachers' genuine love and respect for the children were evident. But families' allegiance resulted more from pride at being part of the Capital Children's Museum than from affection for the MELC. Neither resistant nor enthusiastic, they, along with funders and most other visitors, were satisfied without understanding how much more a preschool could offer.

REGGIO–AN INSPIRATION

In March 1992—27 months after the MELC opened—I visited the schools in Reggio Emilia, Italy. The sophistication of their practices was immediately obvious. The beauty of their environments was overwhelming; the teachers' and children's competence was powerful; the purposefulness of each item and action was evident. I had never seen or imagined such schools before. There, theories we only espoused were robustly practiced. By the third day of my visit, I determined that, as far as possible, the Reggio Approach should guide what the MELC would become.

Uninformed critics asked what schools for children in northern Italy had to do with children in inner-city America: as it turned out, everything! Economically disadvantaged children are often stereotyped as deficient. Reggio schools, in contrast, believe all children are rich, strong, and powerful. The Reggio ideas of listening to children and drawing in families provided the links to our children's power in being exuberant, to their families' richness in experience, and to their culture's strength in persevering. With the Reggio schools as exemplars, I felt confident we could overcome our failure to date to develop an innovative program and could finally begin to live up to the ambitious word *model* in our name. What impressed me about the Reggio schools is described in Chapter 2.

The Reggio Schools

Children construct their own intelligence. The adult must provide activities and context, but most of all must be able to listen. Children need proof that adults believe in them. Their three great desires are to be listened to, to understand, and to demonstrate that they are exactly what we expect.

Loris Malaguzzi

When I visited the schools in Reggio Emilia for the first time in March 1992, I was most impressed by the children's immense competence. Their reasoning, evident in all their work, reflects Reggio educators' fundamental belief that children are *rich, strong,* and *powerful.* This belief drives *how* they teach and *what* they teach, and rests on a system that is highly organized with precise and consistent teaching practices. Altogether, it elicits immense competence in the teachers as well as the children.

Reggio practices form a well-integrated system. In systems theory, or *cybernetics,* control rests equally in all parts of a system; if one part is affected, all are. Thus you cannot focus on one aspect of Reggio schools without also including all the others. Because print is linear, however, I must describe Reggio practices one at a time, asking readers to remember they are inextricably linked. My descriptions reflect my cultural perspective and the limited ability of words to convey a richly layered, dynamic approach.

Much has been written about the Reggio schools. In this chapter I focus on how the following essential characteristics beget the children's and teachers' competence:

- Fully recognizing children's potential
- Working in small groups—children among themselves as well as with their teachers
- Making space and time integral to how the environment is organized
- Defining each teacher's roles as researcher, constructor of the educational experience, and collaborator with colleagues and children
- Integrating a studio (*atelier*) and a studio teacher (*atelierista*) in each school and a mini-*atelier* in each classroom
- Observing, documenting, and revisiting children's work
- Fully engaging families
- Providing for teachers' continuing development equally with children's
- Encouraging the hundred languages to flourish in each child

REALIZING CHILDREN'S POTENTIAL

In La Villetta, a school for 3-to 6-year-olds, I was fascinated by one long wall in the 4-year-olds' room. It was covered by panels of children's work titled "Primary Recognition: Verbal, Graphic, Photographic" and subtitled "A Trip Around the Body: First Hypotheses, First Analyses, First Representations." One panel, titled "The Body in Movement," contained many children's drawings of skillfully executed, fully articulated body parts in various positions. As precise and insightful as the drawings were the children's comments, also on the panel:

> When I move my body, I pull my legs up like I want to run.
> The body moves because it has to move. If it didn't, it would be like a mannequin and it couldn't do anything.
> It's the muscles that make legs move. They make them lift up so you can jump, run, kick a ball.

Observing a group of five children, I realized what had stimulated the competent drawings and comments (see Figures 2.1 and 2.2):

FIGURE 2.1. Children learn about shadows and movement through shadow play. Photo of a girl turning a cartwheel from *Everything Has a Shadow Except Ants*, © Preschool and Infant-toddler Centers—Istituzione of the Municipality of Reggio Emilia, published by Reggio Children (1990).

FIGURE 2.2. Children's accurate drawings reflect their understanding of how their bodies move. Child's drawing of a figure doing a somersault from *Everything Has a Shadow Except Ants*, © Preschool and Infant-toddler Centers—Istituzione of the Municipality of Reggio Emilia, published by Reggio Children (2002).

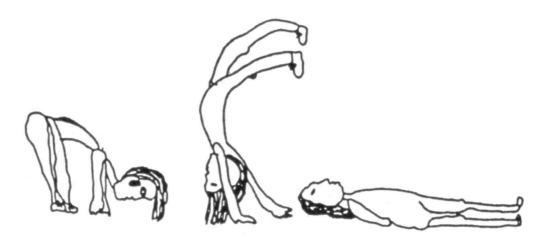

"Luca, Luca, so far . . ."
"Higher! Higher!"
"We'll fly!"
"Luca, jump farther!"

Squeals of delight, shrieks of encouragement, and hilarious laughter accompanied exuberant running and boisterous chasing. The children climbed a ladder, leapt off the top, fell tumbling onto a mat, raced after each other, comparing distances, instigating longer jumps, calling themselves the Climbing Astronauts. During my visit, I watched as they expended enormous energy, conquered a physical challenge, mastered the art of climbing, perhaps overcame a fear of heights. They had created a game, formed rules, put language to use, competed, and collaborated.

The game continued for an hour, while 20 other children, absorbed in various pursuits, were quiet and oblivious, as were the teachers. The single classroom contained hilarity and concentrated activity simultaneously. The teachers neither quieted the children, nor asked them to give others a turn, nor interrupted.

Organizing Precisely

The teachers had designed the climbing apparatus, aware that boisterousness could ensue if children chose it freely. The teachers knew that one aspect of competence is mastery of your body, that movement is a powerful form of expression—for Howard Gardner (1983), an "intelligence"—and that young children must move when *they* want to. Thus, they did not relegate movement to the playground or gym, but structured the environment to reflect their belief that the "environment is a third teacher." In practice this means they trust the environment as much as they trust one another, and create a three-member team from two teachers and an environment. Their painstaking organization results in environment-guided activity that is as valuable as teacher-guided activity.

Reggio educators are researchers, students, and orchestrators of children's competence. They design environments with great forethought, considering every item's placement, size, color, light, and proximity to other areas and to the outdoors. Everything is purposeful—discussed, debated with other teachers, tested, and refined over decades. Thus whatever children use is something their teachers know can increase their competence.

The Astronauts' physical activity was neither random nor isolated, but was the foundation for the competent drawings and comments. Because they had experienced movement, observed the movement of others, and, guided by competent teachers, had explored it thoroughly, they drew and wrote about their movements with intimate knowledge. The children's lifelike drawings and explicit comments reflected their teachers' precision in organizing the environment.

Choosing Consistent Pedagogy

The belief in children's potential was evident in what teachers chose to supervise or to leave unsupervised. Ten American educators explored the park adjoining La Villetta to observe the outcome of the complex project Amusement Park for Birds, which was visited by many Americans and documented in a video by George Forman (1994). The project had a long history evolving from the children's desire to please the birds, who were regular visitors to their park, by building them amusements.

An assortment of colorful, intricate devices covered the half acre: fountains, water wheels, ponds, bird houses, perches where birds could feed, and observation platforms the children had cleverly disguised to blend into the trees. From these children watched the birds through binoculars. Mechanics, physics, technology, design, and empathy had gone into the planning and execution, along with politics and persuasion. The project had started with four children, 5- and 6-year-olds, and eventually spread throughout the school, drawing in parents and even townspeople.

Some members of our delegation observed two children on a bird observation platform as one almost stabbed another with a trowel. No teacher was present to intervene, but a third child did, sharply reproved the aggressor, and took away the tool. An adult could not have done a better job of addressing the potentially dangerous situation. One member of our delegation considered it a weakness in the Reggio Approach that such an episode could occur without adult supervision; the rest concurred with the Reggio educators that such experiences can be mediated effectively by children. It was an example of teachers choosing to let children solve difficult problems on their own, in this case in the area of interpersonal relationships.

The experience reminded me of a Reggio video shown at the November 1991 annual conference of the National Association for the Education of Young Children (NAEYC). A child, setting the table for lunch, purposely smashed china plates, sending pottery shards flying. The audience bombarded the presenter, *pedagogista* Tiziana Filippini: "You use china? You let children carry china? How could you allow this to continue! You cut the footage where you stepped in, didn't you?"

Tiziana's responses grew more incredulous, her final impatient "No!" rising three octaves. Children, not teachers, had resolved the problem by convincing the child to stop smashing plates. Reggio teachers believe that children on the scene can resolve an incident more effectively than a teacher who was not present. Because they are not shielded from something that might be difficult or even dangerous, children hone their competence on situations that are truly challenging, a pedagogical choice that might make Americans uncomfortable.

Reggio teachers support the development of children's competence by explicitly teaching techniques. For example, three children were constructing a complex paper structure, a kitchen aide with them. One tried to cut a thin wire, essential to the construction, but couldn't wield the wire cutter. Silently the aide intervened to demonstrate, taking wire and cutter, holding them so the children could readily observe, and cutting in an exaggerated movement in order to emphasize the technique. Immediately she handed cutter and wire back to the child. In a minute, more wire was needed. This time, the child angled cutter and material correctly, but did not use enough pressure. The aide again intervened, putting her hand over the child's to add pressure. The third time, the child did it himself with no adult intervention.

The interchange was seamless, no comment or praise, no big deal. Yet it was a big deal. A 5-year-old had just mastered a technique requiring an adult tool to cut a potentially dangerous material. The adult's demonstration was intentional—providing the precise help the child needed exactly when needed without lecturing, usurping initiative, or making the child feel inadequate. Reggio teachers choose tools and materials we might not consider appropriate, and support projects we might consider too complex. They work collaboratively with children, not as equals—because clearly teachers can do things children cannot—nor as supervisors, but as team members. The inherent difficulties in the tasks, the teachers' collaboration, the intentional cultivation of technique, and their consistent understanding of when and how to intervene foster the children's competence.

Teaching Masterfully

Reggio teachers respect the wide differences among children in their desire to explore, their acceptance of challenge, and their responses to intervention. Working in a system that values individuality and recognizes children's competence means that, second by second, teachers must use their judgement, always being on their toes to determine the best response to what they observe. Consistently, they strike the right balance between taking the lead and holding back. They "read" each child, size up each situation, and temper their intervention accordingly. But they do it so quickly that it is not apparent they are making choices. In fact, they have habituated this way of acting, just as great athletes or musicians have mastered their techniques as a prerequisite to delivering peak performances. A teacher's response may be swift: a single word, a quick glance, a raised brow. Or it may be expansive: "What a wonderful drawing you made! Can you show it to Fredrico? Can you help him with his drawing? Yours will be an inspiration." Or it may be full of challenge: "Last week your lion looked ferocious! Can you make a lion that I can hear growl? Can he leap off the table?" All responses have an intentionality characteristic of the seasoned actor's ability to select the perfect movement, tone, stance, or expression. Just as the actor "becomes" his character, Reggio teachers are "present" in their teaching every single moment. They are focused, intense, seemingly (but not really) unaware of anything else. They lean toward the child; their eyes engage his; they match rhythm. Their teaching is an exquisite choreography.

When teachers do not trust children's competence or value their differences, when teachers are unclear about the reasons for their own choices, when decisions lack a theoretical underpinning, rules spring up, purportedly for children's protection. Some kindergartens have only fat pencils that cannot sharpen to a point; many don't allow animals; most use plastic rather than glass and china; and most supply blunt-bladed scissors. (Fiskars® makes a scissors with rounded tip and sharp blades.) Such rules are limiting. Schools believe they are protecting children, but actually are saying: We don't trust you; we must protect you from yourself.

Safety is important; however, some practices used in the name of safety prevent children from solving real problems. If adults want to clip a news article and by mistake grab a child's scissors, they would find the tool inadequate. Yet, children are saddled with tools that don't work or standards adults would not tolerate for themselves.

Reggio standards are rooted in beliefs that everyone's rights are equal and that human capacity will grow at any age if people have real challenges to solve. These beliefs unleash children's potential, heighten their individuality, and forge both children's and teachers' competence.

SMALL-GROUP WORK

Reggio schools are perhaps best known for their complex projects undertaken by small groups of children working collaboratively with teachers. In these projects they investigate a material, pursue an interest, or test a hypothesis. Although subject matter varies, projects follow a consistent process and depend on a classroom organized for small-group work. An idea emerges—perhaps from a child, perhaps a teacher—as worth pursuing. First, teachers explore it among themselves to determine if it reflects children's deep interests and has potential to stimulate rich activity. Once they have vetted an idea, they bring it back to the children in the children's own words, drawings, or a teacher's photos. Forming the group who will take part in the project is a strategic process—who is interested, what will entice her, what skills might be required, who possesses those skills. In forming groups, teachers consider every aspect of each child's nature and experience. The next decisions—when to meet, how many should take part, how labor should be divided—are made together by the small group of children and teacher(s).

Projects cover every conceivable subject, for example, what it feels like to be caught in the swell of a crowd, what the sounds of rain look like, how to create a rainbow, how to tell a carpenter the size for a new table, how to construct a life-size dinosaur. The dinosaur project is described by Baji Rankin in a chapter of the book *The Hundred Languages of Children* (1998, pp. 215–237). We might not have believed Rankin's account had our delegation not seen actual results—a large sculpture and mural at Anna Frank School.

Other projects have been described in Reggio publications (Malaguzzi & Filippini, 1991; Spaggiari, Malaguzzi & Dolci, 1990), *The Hundred Languages of*

Children exhibition, Project Zero's book *Making Learning Visible* (Project Zero/Reggio Children, 2001), some issues of the periodical *Innovations* (North American Reggio Emilia Alliance), and elsewhere.

When children and teachers work together, Reggio educators call it *co-collaboration*; it is both a social value and a learning strategy. Co-collaboration can involve tremendous forethought, but can also occur on the fly, teachers intervening quickly if a child needs to perform a skill that is beyond him. The teacher who reaches into a group's paper construction and pinches with enough pressure to make the glue stick is not giving a lesson on "how to"; she is simply furthering the children's aim. American educators, holding different beliefs about appropriate interaction with children, might call it "interference." They might be concerned about stifling creativity, feel that it is somehow cheating to do something for a child, fear rejection if a child does not accept help. But intervention and co-collaboration do not interrupt the flow as interference would.

Usually, a project is only done once, a unique experience in a school's life. Although they might return to the same subject in other years, the perspective is always new because the children are different. If listening and co-collaboration express Reggio schools' spirit, projects are the flesh, sustained by the belief in the value of small-group work.

A TIME–SPACE PARADIGM

In the field of physics Isaac Newton redefined the meaning of time and space, joining them inextricably: "A geometrical task matched a kinetic task: to measure curvature was to find a rate of change. . . . Time and space . . . two abstractions, seemingly disjoint, revealed as cognate" (Gleick, 2003, p. 45). In the field of education Reggio educators redefined the relationship between time and space: to organize the space is to determine how the time will be used. Time is a resource to the same extent that space and materials are resources, as the following examples show.

Timeless Spaces

During our March 1992 visit, Carlina Rinaldi, at the time a *pedagogista*, emphasized that the architecture and furnishings of Reggio preschools are like a language of relationships, shaping and reflecting the pedagogy. The design and selection were the outcome of constant communication among staff, parents, and designers. Numerous glass doors, wall-size windows between rooms, small see-through spaces in the walls, and cleverly placed mirrors encourage relationships to form. "Phones"—funnels connected by tubes that run between rooms—encourage auditory relationships. A mattress and pillows placed behind a curtain encourage a game of peek-a-boo or a quiet tête-à-tête—as social exchange. With small nooks, sofas-for-two, or a comfortable rocker for adults, space is designed to stimulate relationships; time is provided to further them.

Every aspect of architecture and furnishings reflects the importance of the relationship between school and home and school and community. Furniture includes adult-sized chairs or large antique sideboards. Sideboards might contain colored glass bottles or sheaves of wheat, reflecting the region's occupations and offering a glimpse of local culture. These provide a sense of home, which is familiar, but embed the familiar in school, which is new, forming bridges between home and school. Thus the architecture links school with community: Each school's central piazza is a place to gather, gallivant, and engage in other communal pastimes like those that occur in town squares. The architecture also blurs the distinction between inside and out with wall-sized windows, skylights, and atria—a metaphor for open relationships, a core value in Reggio schools.

Wherever possible, the *atelier* and its vast array of materials are visible from the piazza, emphasizing their importance. Huge expanses of wall are covered with panels (called *documentation*), each with title, subtitle, and mix of text, photographs, and children's work. They reveal the program, making the schools' walls seem permeable.

At La Villetta School, our March 1992 delegation had observed a mural so detailed and mature we thought it was commissioned. In fact, it resulted from a collaboration between Giovanni Piazza, La Villetta's *atelierista*, and Amelia Gambetti, then the 5-year-olds' teacher, in a lengthy project in the adjoining park. Over time children had observed the teeming plant and animal life, which they captured from an ant's perspective, and their detailed mural was the project's culmination. A narrow shelf below held wooden or metal noise machines to imitate sounds of particular field creatures. Some made noise when rolled, others when struck, shaken, or strummed. We tried them all, complex in design and execution, the result of children's work over long time periods in highly organized spaces.

Responsive Spaces

Infant school teachers are sensitive to the marked increases in babies' and toddlers' abilities, so they hang objects from the ceiling within reach of babies not yet sitting and different objects for babies sitting but not yet walking. Responding to babies' and toddlers' rapid changes, teachers modify the environments throughout the year to provide new challenges. In September a rubber mat might cover the floor; by midyear a rug and furniture to pull up on are added, with changed items hung from the ceiling. Different objects, like a huge inner tube, appear. Teachers place "treasure baskets" on the floor for babies to explore, each with a collection of related items—brushes with different bristles, variously shaped wooden objects, or assorted small dolls. These collections will also be changed as the year progresses. Mathematical concepts of classification, sets, and similarity are inherent in these careful categorizations (Municipality of Reggio Emilia, 1983, pp. i–iii, 1–12).

Reggio educators believe children should become familiar with the properties —or languages—of different materials while they are learning to speak. So, as soon as babies sit comfortably, they are given paper and brush to explore paint. In these and many other ways space and time nurture competence in infants and babies.

Space, time, and the environment, including the people and objects in it, are all orchestrated. The result is a program that produces competence in all participants along many dimensions of human capacity.

REDEFINING TEACHING

Burnout is an issue in early education because of the energy required to work with young children and the drudgery of some preschool routines. Americans are skeptical when they learn there is no burnout in Reggio schools. The reason is the difference in teachers' roles. Reggio teachers are researchers, designers, and orchestrators. They construct environments to stimulate rich and related experiences, they orchestrate those experiences, and conduct research on what the experiences reveal about children. Teachers do not burn out because they themselves, not a separate curriculum committee or remote state board, set the agenda for what to pursue to further their own research.

The Right Ratio

Malaguzzi told our delegation (March 1992) that having two teachers in every class is vital to the role of teacher as researcher. A new teacher begins by working alongside a teacher with 15 or more years experience. Thus the new teacher has an immediate, continuous role model, a colleague also created through the work, as the new teacher herself will be. These two teach together daily for many years, working with the same children and families, sharing every experience, discussing hundreds of ideas, arguing about interpretations, influencing one another. The experienced teacher is role model, discussant, debater, and coach for the novice. Minute by minute, directly and indirectly, the experienced teacher shapes the new teacher's skills, helping create the competent teacher who the novice becomes.

At the same time, the new teacher provides the experienced one with a fresh viewpoint, challenging the mature teacher's perspective with new ideas, asking questions that provoke the older teacher to explain, rethink, offer reasons, and examine her teaching through new eyes. The process of give-and-take and the responsibility of acting as mentor renew the experienced teacher, keep her on her toes, and extend her competence.

The Art of Listening

At La Villetta, our guide, Amelia Gambetti, teacher of the 5- and 6-year-olds, emphasized:

> We do not have recipes! The children are the teachers in our school
> and we, the teachers, learn every day. I used to think of the teacher
> as a boss with solutions. No! We listen to the children's opinions,
> and build activities based on what we hear.

She described the challenge of grasping in a single conversation what a child wants to say: For example, teachers could easily have overlooked children's comments when, decorating the gym for a celebration and quickly daunted by the huge space, they asked: "Do you think we could invent a machine to blow up balloons? We're tired of doing that! A machine would save our strength." But the teacher heard and spoke with Giovanni Piazza, the *atelierista*. They agreed that if the children wanted to make such a machine, they saw no reason they could not, and children and teachers together actually built one that generated a strong current of air. A wind machine was the farthest thing from the teacher's mind; on her mind was to listen carefully.

Autonomy in Teaching

Reggio teachers function with the kinds of autonomy and support that typify advanced investigations in science or technology. As doctors listen to sounds in their patients' bodies for clues to possible treatments, Reggio teachers listen to what children say for clues to directions for their research. Some teachers have tried to determine whether there are intrinsic differences between the exploratory behavior of male and female toddlers; others have helped children exploit physical and metaphysical aspects of shadows, or aesthetic and scientific properties of light. Still others have explored the boundaries of children's abilities by constructing large bridges, fabricating a working wing of a giant bird, inventing systems for measurement, or creating techniques to describe subtle color differences. These teachers are keen observers of how children's reactions reveal what they know and how they think. Such are the pursuits of the teacher-researcher, not following a preset curriculum but engaged every minute in constructing the educational experience. What the children learn beyond specific facts or skills is an attitude and approach to learning: to question, hypothesize, research, try, revise, collaborate, and persevere.

ATELIERISTA AND *ATELIER*

The *atelierista* (studio teacher) and *atelier* (studio) are central to Reggio practice. The *atelier* has excellent lighting, plentiful work space, places for display, systems to store materials, tools, and finished work—full, but not cluttered. The *atelierista* and *atelier* are vital to what Reggio educators call "the hundred languages of children," which in turn are integral to how the children become competent.

Role of the *Atelierista*

Every school has an *atelierista* who is an expert in one or more art forms. Not responsible for a class, the *atelierista* works with all teachers and children. These studio teachers are skilled with materials, and their expertise in production is evident throughout the school. Their role is complex, sometimes suggesting projects to teachers and children, often acting as the catalyst to move a project along. Each runs a large *atelier*, but can also be found in the classrooms.

During our visit to the *atelier* at La Villetta School, *atelierista* Giovanni Piazza's own drawings were everywhere: Beautiful colored-pencil renderings of intricate machinelike assemblies straddled the boundary between realistic and fanciful. Objects in Giovanni's *atelier* appealed to the sense of sight or touch, like machines, some complicated, proposing kinesthetic exploration. Each *atelier* is a personal space reflecting its *atelierista*'s particular interests and visual and spatial style

The partnership between teachers and *atelierista*, often together for 20 years, frequently sparks projects as they grapple from their different viewpoints with what children's words and actions mean. Such teamwork guards against overlooking or misinterpreting a child's remark—something that could easily happen—and enhances each one's competence.

Function of the *Atelier*

A huge worktable dominates the longer side of Giovanni's L-shaped *atelier*. Low shelves line the walls. They contain paper, organized by size, texture, and color and a variety of paints, pencils, markers, pens, and inks. Taller shelves contain a library of books on art and design; others contain woodworking tools. Like a graphic designer's office, the *atelier* is visually intriguing. A group working on a project goes to the *atelier* together when they need expert guidance or resources. An *atelier* is not used like the American art room with groups going at predetermined times for teacher-prepared activities. Rather, activities percolate up from the children themselves and their collaboration with their teachers on projects. The *atelier* facilitates deep exploration of materials or meets projects' emerging needs, supports the partnerships of *atelierista* and teachers, and always reflects children's involvement in projects important to them. The children's copious work, complete or in progress, is intricate and detailed, reminiscent of works by Miro, Tingay, or Picasso.

Importance of Materials

Materials are important to children; they are the means through which their hundred languages develop. Giovanni related that early on, as the studio teachers began to explore and define their role, they realized that all teachers need skill with materials, both to convey their needs to the *atelierista* and to fulfill the potential in their collaboration with children. So in 1982 a mini-*atelier* was added to every classroom. Consequently, teachers' roles expanded to involve increasingly sophisticated use of materials.

For 3 years, the *atelieristas* concentrated on exploring single types of material, trying to understand the potential in each. They did this for paper, clay, string, wire, and hose. Giovanni showed us their inventory of verbs denoting ways to *act* on paper: smooth, crumple, roll up, fold up, tear up, roll into a ball, cut out, twist, trace, print, wrap up, unwrap, scratch, engrave, place on, take to pieces, reassemble, construct, draw, color, cut, cut up, interlace, wet, soak, punch, bunch, rub out, fit in, duplicate, and decorate. Another list of verbs denoted things to *do* with paper: hide, sound, fly about, blow, set a fire, set fire to, stand up, cover oneself up, roll, lay down, tread on, mold, paint, graph, chew, bite, lick, and rub. In response to teachers' requests, much paper comes from homes: wax, computer, and construction paper; lined, ruled, typing, and tracing paper; newsprint; shiny, transparent, and contact paper; aluminum foil, parchment, cardboard, cookie cups, and candy wrappers.

Results of this research on paper are evident everywhere. Toddlers had arrived one morning at the infant school Il Girotondo to find the piazza floor covered in paper for them to mark on or tear. In an exploration carried out in different classes children had wrapped tiny objects in a multitude of papers, then displayed the collection on a panel. Each child has his own light box, made from a shoe box, with an array of two-dimensional silhouettes and other paper props. Four-year-olds make three-dimensional origami. Older children weave paper strips on small looms, 6"–12" square. A small group made a 4' × 4' weaving, called "Summer," from a huge variety of paper strips.

Story of a Project

In Giovanni'a *atelier*, a group of six 5- and 6-year-olds was putting the final decorative elements on the machine they'd built to save their strength blowing up balloons. The project went on for 40 days, with 30 children eventually joining. First, children and teachers researched machines together. From the *atelier* came tape recorders, cameras, materials, tools, and Giovanni's knowledge. They made many sketches. Five children presented ideas to one another for how the machine might work. The group discussed which ideas were better and which to eliminate. They cut and glued copies of their drawings, merging the features they considered best into one machine, abandoning what they considered weak. Then they made many prototypes. Now it was obvious why Giovanni's *atelier* had so many machines.

The result—a truly fantastic wind machine imaginatively decorated—stood like a gaudy carnival attraction at the entry to Giovanni's *atelier*. The complexity of the problem, the elegance of the solution, the working machine itself belied the inventors' ages, but testified to their competence.

Every *atelier* proclaims that work of great consequence takes place, that many things have been made and many more will be. The *atelierista*'s capacities and wealth of materials are integral to everything that happens throughout the school and to developing a hundred languages.

OBSERVING, DOCUMENTING, REVISITING

In March 1992 at Arcobaleno School our delegation's attention was arrested by the extensive number of photographs with text assembled on panels, which Carlina called *documentation*. Panels hang everywhere in all Reggio schools in carefully chosen locations, each panel's layout thoughtfully designed. Amelia called them "a school's memory." They are evidence of a trio of practices that was unique to Reggio—observing, documenting, and revisiting. Carlina told us, "We dedicate a lot of space, physical and mental, to memory." When panels are removed eventually to make room for new ones, they are photographed as a memory bank of the school's past.

Purpose of Documentation

Documentation reminds staff and children of what they have done. For parents and other visitors, it reveals a school's daily life and history. Documentation contains photographs, children's work and words, and teachers' descriptions of an experience. In infant centers, documentation includes photos hung low where babies can see them and toddlers can talk about them. Teachers hang notes and photographs in transparent envelopes, one for each child. They continually update notes and often add new photos. Thus highlights of each child's year accumulate, and eventually are gathered into diaries and given to parents.

Documentation is not passive like wallpaper, but is integral to the program; it is not only the story of a school's evolving life but also a force in that evolution. Teachers use documentation to keep themselves and the children focused. When a teacher picks up on the children's interests, she may mount a blank panel with a provocative statement or question suggesting a direction for an activity. As the activity proceeds, she selects those photos, text, or examples of children's work that reflect critical decision points or discoveries. In Amelia's words, "Teachers are administrative assistants to the ideas of children."

A panel may begin as the project begins. Text comes from teachers' notes or tape recordings, which they review together in lengthy after-school meetings, searching for themes, determining which remarks suggest projects, or which should be titles or quotes on a panel. These meetings include lively, often heated discussion; the choice of every word and image is a cause for deliberation and debate because the teachers know that documentation keeps children focused and triggers next projects.

Documentation is not pretty pictures of engaged children. Rather, it captures the thinking process: What motivated them to begin, continue, change direction? What were the breakthroughs, the pivotal remarks or actions? How did they solve the problem? The goal is to enable whoever reads a panel to understand what the children attempted and how they went about it, to see stimulus, process, and outcome (see Figure 2.3).

The teachers are excellent photojournalists, knowing what will reveal the intent and keep the story moving. Because teachers prepare documentation as an activity moves along, what happened recently—yesterday or last week—is fresh in everyone's minds and tremendously motivating to the children. Panels are the stories of stories being created as life at school proceeds. They are self-reflexive, like the picture on the old-fashioned cereal box of a man holding a cereal box with a picture of himself holding a cereal box with the same picture, and so on and on.

How Adults Use Documentation

When teachers are in the process of considering what might happen next, they themselves *revisit* a panel to read a project's emerging story and debate next steps. They search the panel for fertile directions, speculating about possible outcomes in a process charged with discussion, disagreement, and eventual consensus.

Documentation is also part of teachers' professional development. When a group of teachers revisits a project through its documentation, these colleagues' perspectives—their reactions and opinions—are valuable feedback for the teachers involved in the project. Group members stimulate one another to rethink what they did, what was good, how it might have differed. Families use documentation to observe their children and, reciprocally, it attracts families to the school. Because documentation is used to plan for the classroom as well as for teacher education and families, it is critically important to the system.

Giovanni emphasized to us how photos on the panels aid the memory—of children, teachers, and families. He explained the unique joining of perspectives: *atelierista* with artist's knowledge of materials and craftsperson's understanding of their potential; teachers with their shared experiences over long years together; 3-year periods with the same children and families. Documentation provides so

FIGURE 2.3. Not *art for art's sake*, but art for *thinking's* sake. Child's drawing of a figure and its shadows under two lampposts from *Everything Has a Shadow Except Ants*, © Preschool and Infant-toddler Centers—Istituzione of the Municipality of Reggio Emilia, published by Reggio Children (1990).

lively a portrayal of the children's endeavors that, even at night long after they've gone, their presence fills the rooms. As Amelia told us, documentation is "a window into the mind of our schools."

FAMILY PARTICIPATION

The numerous ways families are drawn into the school are as deliberate as every other practice. Reggio teachers believe that families help to construct the educational experience.

Relationship building begins in a school's entryway, which is literally an avenue for communication. In entry halls to the school and to each classroom, pages of information communicate with families. Each page is strategically placed, thoughtfully designed. Cristina Bondavalli, a former Reggio teacher turned administrator, describes classrooms' entryways:

The entryway of each room should offer to parents . . . something that gives ideas about what the teachers and children are doing. They should find their own children there, perhaps through notebooks or journals of the teachers. They should also find information and images of what is happening inside the room and how the group is forming. A journal prepared by the teachers should communicate a sort of panoramic view, . . . the changes that are taking place in that room or section. (quoted in Gandini, 2001, p. 59)

Comfortable furniture invites parents to stay. Their children's photographs draw them to examine the walls.

The school is the next circle as a baby's world enlarges. Teachers construct the experience with families. The summer before their child begins school, a family visits. Parents are expected to remain at school as their infant becomes acclimated, a period called *inserimento*. The root *inserire* means "to connect," and reflects Reggio educators' view of the three-way bond between child, teacher, and parents. Older children's parents visit several times before a child enters school. Each receives a specially prepared book to fill with information; it acquaints the teachers with the child, and whets the family's appetite for school.

Once a family becomes part of the school, there are many avenues for involvement. Virtually all parents attend meetings where teachers discuss what happens in the classroom; large numbers attend celebrations and festivals that they and the teachers organize. Because they value their schools, families are effective political advocates on the schools' behalf. Parents' involvement reflects their particular interests. Some host visitors, others collect or prepare materials. Parents who work with their hands construct equipment or collaborate in activities using materials. For example, the exhibit of weavings at Anna Frank School resulted from collaboration between children and parents.

Schools are not a substitute for families but rather, as Carlina explained, "a system of connections and interaction among children, home, and school," organized around children's and families' relationships with a school and its teachers.

SUPPORTING TEACHERS FULLY

The formal name of the Reggio schools is the Department of Infant and Toddler Centers and Kindergartens. The organization evolved as a system to enhance teachers' full potential, not only children's. Finding adequate resources has often meant becoming deeply involved in politics at local, regional, and federal levels. One result is that an *assessore* (councillor), one of 12 elected members of the Town Council, represents the Reggio schools' interests, insuring their concerns are heard at the city's highest government level.

A key facet of professional development is the employment of various special personnel, for example the *pedagogista*. The only remotely comparable American position is curriculum specialist. But a *pedagogista*'s expertise far exceeds curriculum. Patrizia Ghedini, director of childhood services for Emilia Romagna, the regional government, says the role of *pedagogista* promotes "the growth of a *culture of childhood* in local communities" (Ghedini, 2001, p.45, emphasis in original). Each works with four schools, not teaching, but facilitating classroom teachers' work in various ways—collaborating on a project or panel, joining parent meetings, consulting about behavior problems, participating in selecting new staff, planning professional education activities.

Other specialized departments and personnel include the Handicapped Coordinator and personnel who are skilled at providing one-on-one assistance for children with disabilities. (It is interesting to note that children without grandparents are also considered handicapped, reflecting Reggio educators' appreciation for multigenerational family relationships.) In addition, there is a Theater Workshop, a Center for Educational Research, an Office for Educational Exchanges, and Reggio Children, new in 1994, "an international center for the defense and development of the rights and potential of infants and children" (L. Malaguzzi, statement at a meeting, June 1993). Each entity has its own professional and administrative staff.

The high priority given to ongoing professional development is reflected in teachers' schedules, which include time to prepare the classroom, meet with parents, and attend professional meetings. For example, in 1990–91, of 36 hours per week, 6 hours (over 15%) were allocated to "up-to-dating" meetings, social management, planning, workshops, administrative meetings, cultural enterprises, preparation of materials, talks, and other nonteaching tasks (Municipality of Reggio Emilia, 1990). Up-to-dating meetings have an intellectual-philosophical content comparable to presentations at scientific conferences. Ongoing education for preschool teachers in Italy, especially the northern regions where Reggio Emilia is located, reflects the populace's high regard for the profession of teaching.

THE HUNDRED LANGUAGES OF CHILDREN

The words *hundred languages* are central to the Reggio philosophy. Malaguzzi first used them in a poem, then as the name of extensive traveling exhibitions. To Reggio educators, *languages* means "facility in many media," including human exchange. The word *hundred* is a term of convenience; there could be several hundred.

The *Atelier* and the Hundred Languages

Work in the *atelier*—in clay, sand, wire, wood, paint, and fabric—testifies that children can use hundreds of languages. A glass wall in Diana School's piazza offers a view into the *atelier*. There, in the school closest to the old city, the role of *atelierista* was partly defined. From the nearby administrative offices, Malaguzzi visited frequently. Vea Vecchi, *atelierista* from Diana's inception, told our March 1992 delegation that their long dialogues over many years helped shape the *atelier*'s purpose, the *atelierista*'s role, and the concept of "a hundred languages."

One panel in Diana School's *atelier* read, "Children teach each other."

"What do you know how to make with clay?"

"I know everything."

"I am making snails."

"... a bridge."

"... a table."

"... a little chair."

"I'm going to give this chocolate to Luis."

"... a tank; I'm going to roll it on the table."

"... little balls."

Another was titled "Multiwire Shapes" and subtitled "The Play of Wire, the Play of Shapes." A nearby panel, "Becoming Something Else *(Travestimenti)* with Wire," questioned, "How many different things can you make this become?" Italians call such questions *provocations*. The Italian word *provocare* connotes eliciting response and wonder or urging forward, not negatively quarrelsome as in English. This particular *provocazione* (provocation) yielded mobiles hung with a vast array of attractive miniature objects and intricate wire figures. Other provocations stimulated highly articulated clay models, rich weavings, remarkable drawings, huge murals, and complex assemblages more typical of mature artists than 4-to 6-year-olds.

The Hundred Languages in Action

The following episode illustrates the hundred languages. The context is a full morning in Diana School's 4-year-old room during my visit in February 1993. Many children had arrived by 8:30, early-comers putting away their coats, a few choosing materials, most chatting together. Shortly after 9, they gathered on wooden steps. The teacher passed out quartered oranges. As they sucked the fruit, the teacher greeted each child, welcoming a stuffed toy, a few long discussions, most short. Then the children quickly dispersed to tables or areas, most in previously formed groups, some remaining all morning with their initial choice, others changing.

The classroom was already prepared. One table had wire and tiny objects for a mobile. The light table had materials for collages—markers, glue, and translucent papers, mainly greens and yellows, and intriguing bits of other materials in the same colors. End products are beautiful in part because teachers preselect materials with particular qualities like reflectivity or color blend. Another table had clay, tools to cut and shape it, and stands to support figures. The table in the mini-*atelier* was covered with white quadrille paper on which were a large triangulated ruler, other rulers, and jars with multitudes of pens and pencils.

After half an hour, four boys, who hadn't settled into anything, entered a small room adjoining the mini-*atelier*, closing the door behind them. "Mischief!" I thought, expecting the teacher to follow, or at least open the door. She did neither, although the four had been unsettled to the point of disrupting others. The morning passed with everyone becoming highly engrossed. The four never emerged and toward noon the door was still closed. All this time the teacher had been with the same small group in the mini-*atelier*, unable to see into the small room. No longer able to contain my curiosity, I asked if I could go into the small room. The teacher motioned me ahead. Because the room was too small for the door to remain ajar, I closed it behind me, leaving me alone with the boys, who appeared not to notice me.

The room was like a large storeroom, the space packed tight and well organized. One wall had floor-to-ceiling shelving with a horde of accessible supplies. A sand table ran along an adjacent wall. In the middle was a long table. The boys' voices, tinged with pleasure and sounds of productive engagement, filled the room. They had built an elaborate structure, vertical struts anchored in the sand, supporting a "roof," made from a glowing blue metallic sheet. Above floated filmy materials—gauzy fabric, cotton, the means of attachment not visible. "Castles in the air," I fantasized. Under the roof was an array of tubes, sheets of thin wood, and cardboard with other materials stretched between, an intricate, complicated construction. When I entered, two were working at the sand table, the other two at the long table completing a detailed structure of small interconnecting blocks. Suddenly, they burst open the door, excitedly calling the teacher. They wanted to move the block structure into the sand table, but were not sure how without destroying it. The teacher delved into the shelves and retrieved a large, sturdy board. Then, closing the door behind her, she returned to the mini-*atelier*. I continued observing.

The block builders, needing help, interrupted their friends at the sand table, directing them to steady the board even with the edge of the long table. Then, with utmost care, they nudged the structure onto the board. Together, all four lowered it to the sand table, only to discover there was not enough space. At that point, the teacher announced lunch. Carefully, the four lifted the board with the block structure back to its table, negotiating with the teacher how to leave everything in place. She resolved the problem by making a sign indicating that no one should disturb either structure. As the children left for lunch, they talked excitedly about the next steps.

Everywhere I had seen evidence of the hundred languages: schools equipped so adults can pursue their own interests and share them with children who become well versed in using materials. Soundproof music rooms, a great assortment of climbing structures, jeweler's gold scales, up-to-date computers, professional drums—all there to foster children's and adults' competence in varied pursuits. Schoolyards resemble elaborate parks. Fanciful water sculptures and ingenious water-play structures befit the best children's museums. Little comes from school supply catalogues. Equipment is made by teachers and parents who are competent in music, physics, sculpture, engineering, design, or construction.

But the phrase *hundred languages* has another meaning—the perspectives of others. Learning what others know and how they think comes about through small-group activity. When children make things together with others, who include teachers, they observe others' different abilities up close. This promotes conversation, which in turn challenges and ultimately changes each one's own contribution. By bumping their ideas against others' theories and their capabilities against others' skills, they enlarge their own perspective. In Reggio terms, they learn to speak a hundred languages.

SUMMARY

What one might think would be chaos with the Climbing Astronauts or mischief with the boys in the "storeroom" was purposeful, self-contained activity, sometimes initiated by children, often uninterrupted, without teachers present unless they were collaborators. Activities usually involved a group, was always furthered by the environment, and was long-sustained, continuing for hours or days. It reflected teachers' beliefs in children's potential and showcased the teachers' and children's remarkable competence.

As a serious attempt to convey the workings of complex schools, my words sound ponderous. But when we were there, we could hear the joyous sounds of children's laughter, observe their exuberance, notice their concentration, and feel their affection for each other and their teachers. Words writ large on the huge window into Diana School's *atelier* proclaim: *Niente senza gioia* (Nothing without joy)! Joy is the hallmark of activity in Reggio schools.

The complementary roles of time and space, the teachers' role as researcher-constructor, the *atelier* and *atelierista*, the competence in a hundred languages, the documentation practices, the extensive involvement of families, and the amount of ongoing teacher development are distinctive features of the Reggio system. But, of all these, to me the most remarkable is the core belief in children's potential. I think the gulf separating American and Reggio practices is widest around this issue. Sooner than I imagined, we would test our own beliefs as we began to adapt Reggio practices in the MELC.

CHAPTER 3

Another New Start

If you set out to find new things, you will lose sight of the shore for a very long time.

André Gide

I returned from Reggio in March 1992. The MELC had been open for 27 months. We had two teachers, two assistant teachers, and one aide. Our fifth director was just beginning. Awed by what I had seen in Reggio schools, I determined to adapt their practices for the MELC. I showed the teachers my slides and recounted my visit, and they caught my enthusiasm.

That spring the two assistant teachers, Sonya Shoptaugh (white) and Wendy Baldwin (African American), became cohead teachers. They had lived through the chaos before classroom management procedures were established, and had learned from the third director how to help children develop self-discipline, the prerequisite without which we could not have begun to adapt the Reggio Approach.

It was a terrible blow when, after only 6 weeks, the fifth director did not work out. For the first time the care of the environment was slipshod, and parents were complaining about activities in the classroom. In particular, children were encouraged to act out stories so realistically, it was inappropriate. We were all upset. Yet, the teachers looked terrified when I told them we would, once again, be changing leadership.

In this chapter, describing another new start, I examine my own leadership of the MELC, explain how the teachers began to learn about Reggio schools and how I rebuilt the environment. I also take stock of where we were in the last months of spring 1992.

A CEO-STYLE DIRECTOR

Although I was president of The National Learning Center and executive director of the Capital Children's Museum, Options School, and the MELC, I took on daily responsibility as the MELC's director, knowing that at that moment—mid-April 1992, after five directors—consistent leadership was essential. I told the teachers their concerns would have my immediate attention; we would meet twice weekly, more if they needed. I feared that, after the initially rocky years, they would resign. To my immense relief, all stayed. They were as intrigued as I to study the Reggio practices. Aware of the museum's stature, they trusted my ability to initiate programs, respected my drive, and were willing to live with my time pressures.

Those pressures were immense. I ran TNLC, comprised of the large and multifaceted museum and the Options School, a dropout-prevention junior high school program for 100 students, new each year, sent to us by D.C. Public Schools principals as, in their words, their hundred worst. I was also overseer, but not yet daily director, of the problem-filled MELC. In addition, I was involved in numerous teacher education initiatives and was responsible for TNLC's administrative staff. I set the vision, implemented new programs, and oversaw established ones. I also selected key staff, raised $3 million annually, and controlled the budget. Of all the programs initiated during my 20-year tenure at TNLC, I considered the MELC most important. Recent research seemed to be shouting, "Time for a breakthrough in preschool education!" If the MELC did not become exemplary, I would close it; we did not need to showcase mediocrity.

Theory Oriented

For anyone who stepped from the elevator into the MELC, our mission statement, proclaiming new theories of learning, dominated the vestibule. Gardner (1983) represented the neurological perspective, that there is a physiological basis—actual activity in particular parts of the brain—for intelligences identified in his Multiple Intelligence theory. Feuerstein (1991) represented the social constructivist perspective (following Vygotsky), that learning is fundamentally social; the theory of the Mediated Learning Experience (MLE) holds that without human mediation, optimum cognitive function will not develop. Piaget represented constructivist theory; his idea that materials and environment are vital in human development was inherent in Montessori's work, which we also acknowledged.

Gardner's and Feuerstein's theories are based on multifaceted research from many fields—neurology, sociology, anthropology, psychology, and the new sciences of chaos, complexity, and systems theory. Reggio practices reflect these theories' convergence and thus constitute a leading edge in school practice. In starting anew I hoped the MELC could make Reggio practices flourish in an American inner-city preschool.

Time Pressured

I became director of the MELC, but in reality, as president of TNLC, I was consumed by issues throughout the organization. Aside from our meetings and being on call, I had little time to work with the teachers as a collaborator. Outside those meetings, my communication tended to be memos, usually written late at night as I responded to daily piles on my desk. My memos read like fiats—"Use," "Make," "Purchase," "Develop," "Put," "Find"— exactly opposite to the Reggio Approach, in which practices evolve through mutual exploration, lengthy discussion, and frequent group reflection. For example, on April 29, 1992, I wrote this memo to the teachers:

> Three new things have been introduced recently without adequate
> planning. Until we develop them, their usefulness will be sorely
> limited. As an exercise in preparing the environment, we will take

these three things—and a fourth described below—and develop them fully.

Housekeeping Area:

I will instruct Frank [head of museum construction] to make a unit like they use for dress-up clothes in Reggio. In the meantime collect attractive clothes.

Shop the Goodwill stores for interesting dress-up objects. Think creatively. Give [TNLC] staff a notice, and put an item in our newsletter requesting clothes and household items of interest and beauty. . . . The key words in developing this area are *awe* and *wonder*.

Order will be essential. Things heedlessly put on shelves . . . get broken!

The memo reflected my dismay. The MELC's environment had deteriorated. The school was ugly and cluttered with many broken items, and the staff seemed unaware of the conditions. But how I expressed my dismay was not constructive. Fortunately the teachers hung on. Evidently, Reggio's allure and their motivation overcame my graceless memos.

My first steps in spring 1992 were to candidly discuss the recent difficulties so we could put them behind us, then share what I knew about the Reggio approach. Together we read articles about Reggio and Italian early education by Lella Gandini, the official Reggio liaison to the United States who was among the first to introduce Reggio ideas in America, and by Rebecca New. We looked at slides I had taken in Reggio, probed their meaning, and considered how to do what they portrayed.

INTRODUCING REGGIO

The teachers' first exposure to Reggio was my secondhand accounts from exposure I had had over several years, especially from my visit in March 1992. I was glad to be guiding the teachers because I reveled in sharing the new ideas I so admired. In June Sonya, Wendy, and I attended a multi-day workshop given by three Reggio educators for the MELC teachers to receive some firsthand information.

Secondhand Accounts

My first introduction to Reggio had been in 1984, when George Forman, an American who early embraced the Reggio philosophy, began to lobby for the Capital Children's Museum to host Reggio's *Hundred Languages* exhibit (which we finally did in 1989). My next involvement, in 1988, was designing and attempting to fund a classroom-behind-glass as a hands-on museum exhibition to accompany Reggio's *Hundred Languages* exhibit. Hoping to arouse public interest in Reggio, CCM hosted lectures by Gandini, Forman, and Pamela Houk, arts educator and museum curator. In 1990 CCM hosted a public session with *pedagogiste* Tiziana Filippini and Carlina Rinaldi on the *Hundred Languages* exhibit. Its display at CCM coincided with NAEYC's annual conference. I showed the two *pedagogiste* the new

MELC but, not yet having seen their Reggio schools, did not understand why they weren't excited.

In March 1992 I organized a delegation of Washingtonians to visit Reggio (see Chapter 2). My slides from that visit formed the staff's most vivid introduction. Slides of the environments were the most understandable; in others, none of us could determine the process behind the image. But we could adapt much from the environment, and together made lists of what we most wanted. We wanted everything!

A favorite slide showed a child arranging a large collection of shells while inside a large square pyramid, a structure with clear or colored plexiglass and mirrors all around. Sitting inside, children view the classroom beyond or their constructions inside in a multitude of perspectives and colors, infinite in the mirrors and ephemeral in the hues. The MELC *had* to have a pyramid!

Slides that amazed us but were indecipherable were of wide shelftops containing vast collections of small items, meticulously arranged, each touching surrounding items, completely covering the shelf. They evidenced huge possibilities in range and arrangement of materials. Years later, MELC teacher Jennifer Azzariti said, "This is something I would do, but would never have thought of bringing into the classroom. Color and shape were juxtaposed so fully but so thoughtfully that it was not overwhelming." The shelves reminded her of Victorian curio cabinets.

Many slides captivated us: collections of tiny objects; a wee, fragile dollhouse; a set of realistically detailed, minuscule horses; tubes of every girth and length used for communication, building, or props in shadow play. Children's work reflected richness juxtaposed with richness, and was everywhere—over doorways, covering windows, dangling from ceilings. The variety was staggering, each beautiful item skillfully executed and thoughtfully exhibited. The teachers and I were mesmerized but bewildered—attracted by what we saw, uninformed about how it came to be, unsure how it related to us.

Firsthand Accounts

In June 1992, Sonya, Wendy, and I attended a program on Reggio at Mt. Ida College, Newton Centre, Massachusetts. Between lectures by *pedagogista*, *atelierista*, and teacher, we sat on the grass, designed our parent program, and laid many other plans.

My notes on Carlina Rinaldi's lecture reflect her emphasis on Reggio's view of the child:

> One can consider the child from many perspectives—psychological, educational, the mass media's image, one's own common sense. A dominant theory today is the emphasis on the child's needs and fears, too much so in Reggio educators' opinion, who instead emphasize a child's potential and rights. In Reggio Emilia the image is of a child who is *rich, strong,* and *powerful,* who has *rights,* not simply *needs.*

Carlina provided a structure for talks that followed by Amelia Gambetti and Giovanni Piazza.

Amelia described the teacher's context: facts like the school's layout and teacher-student ratios; how a morning passes in "discussion, drawing, more discussion, the search for materials" as children confront a diversity of problems. Giovanni described the importance of group process, what he called "nonindividual construction." The three lectured together about the collaborative nature of their work, explaining their different roles by describing each one's part in a project: the adults who, Carlina said, "must construct a context in which the child can form relationships"; the teacher who, Amelia stressed, makes sure every day the child goes "to a place I enjoy"; the *atelierista* who, Giovanni emphasized, adds a different perspective.

We knew what we heard was vitally important for what we wanted the MELC to become, and tried to link the lectures to our situation. But the words washed over us, remote from anything we were doing; the points of connection were not obvious, how to begin unclear. At Mt. Ida I realized I had reached the limit of what I could offer the teachers, and approached Amelia to request her help. She answered emphatically, "Impossible!"

The teachers left for summer vacation, and I returned to Washington. My notes and slides from Reggio, reinforced by what I had just heard, would guide me in rebuilding the MELC.

REBUILDING

It was summer 1992. On the fifth floor, far above the Museum's bustle, the MELC was quiet. But the shelves held a noisy hodgepodge, and the furniture was stark in comparison to Reggio's. We could not have predicted the extent of the changes. The MELC floor plan (see Figure 3.1) shows both the size and many of the alterations to the space from the work that summer.

The teachers were gone. Needing a break, they had plans for the summer—Sonya in California, Wendy in North Carolina; had they wanted to stay, we had no funds for stipends. When I had asked if they would object to my working alone on the space, they seemed relieved that I would take this on. They were comfortable because they knew I had designed numerous exhibits for CCM and liked my aesthetic. I was comfortable because I had extensive design experience, control of the budget, and authority as executive director to use the museum's exhibit construction staff and shop facilities. Moreover, as vacation approached, I had reviewed potential changes with the teachers; their strongest desire was to have a dedicated studio. Beyond that, they liked—and wanted—everything they had seen in the slides of Reggio schools.

The space was generous: The MELC spread along a city block, about 3,500 square feet, as large as three sizeable kindergartens. There were numerous large windows, many dormers, two skylights. Rooms varied—some sizeable, others small—a mix of open spaces, small nooks, unexpected turns, and irregularly shaped halls. Bathrooms were large. Wall space was vast. One aspect of the word *model* in our name referred to the amount of space: We hoped the MELC could become a reference for those who advocate more space for early education.

Before making any changes I reorganized the storeroom, the school's resource bank. I discarded anything broken, mismatched, or commercial, then *containerized* and labeled what was left. Next I cleared off the shelves in each room,

FIGURE 3.1. Floor plan, Model Early Learning Center. (Copyright 2004 by archimania, Memphis, TN.)

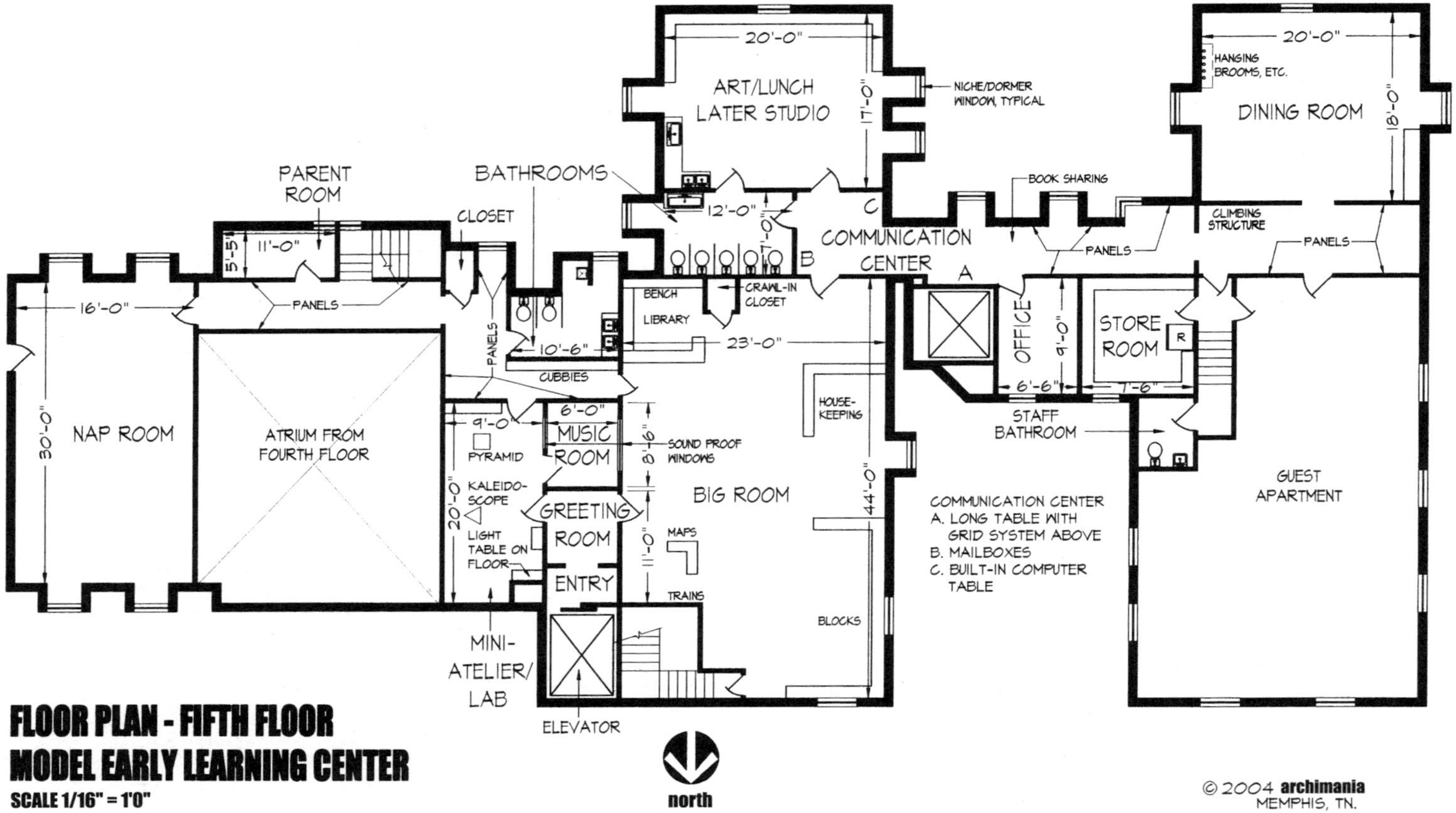

FLOOR PLAN - FIFTH FLOOR
MODEL EARLY LEARNING CENTER
SCALE 1/16" = 1'0"

© 2004 archimania
MEMPHIS, TN.

throwing away what was worn, incorporating anything useful into the storeroom. Empty of all but the furniture, the rooms were easier to design.

Studio

Not even a corner resembled an *atelier*. Pam Houk helped me design the Studio in a room that had been used for art and lunch. She had accompanied our Reggio delegation, so we shared a vision of how the *atelier* should look: huge mirror, storage systems for materials, shelves for children's work, finished and in progress, as well as spaces for portfolios of children's large work and storage systems for small work. There was also a large new sink, light table, and oversized easels. Together we readied it for an *atelierista*—our studio teacher—to fill with materials and take ownership (see Figure 3.2).

Special Spaces

I engaged the Museum's construction shop in building a square pyramid and kaleidoscope for the Lab and in rebuilding a closet in the Big Room to have storage above and a crawl-in nook below. A long jog in a hallway became a Communication Center with built-in table (see Figure 3.3). A grid system above supported objects to entice children to communicate: small papers in a multitude of sizes, colors, weights, textures; assorted envelopes; writing implements with lead and ink, black and colored; fasteners including brads, clips, staples, bands, string,

FIGURE 3.2. Early work in clay and paint. (MELC Studio)

FIGURE 3.3. New Communication Center in leftover hallway space.

ribbon, tape, tacks, glue; tools including scissors, punches, rulers, staplers, sharpeners, erasers. In a nearby jog in the hallway we built a computer table, and on an adjoining wall created a system of mailboxes from Arco bins by adding opaque plexiglass doors—an individual box for each child, adult, and Coco, the MELC's cat.

Music Room

My assistant persuaded a contractor to undertake a major project pro bono, constructing a soundproof music room with huge windows on opposite sides so one could see from the Big Room through the Music Room to the Lab. I equipped it with a sizeable collection of varied African drums, finger pianos, other percussive instruments, and a stand with Montessori bells. A colorful fabric map of Africa covered one wall; a new hanging system for instruments children would make covered another (see Figure 3.4).

Lab

In its new iteration the Lab contained a pyramid, a kaleidoscope, collections of natural objects, and a computer dedicated to software with math and spatial

FIGURE 3.4. Newly built and appointed Music Room.

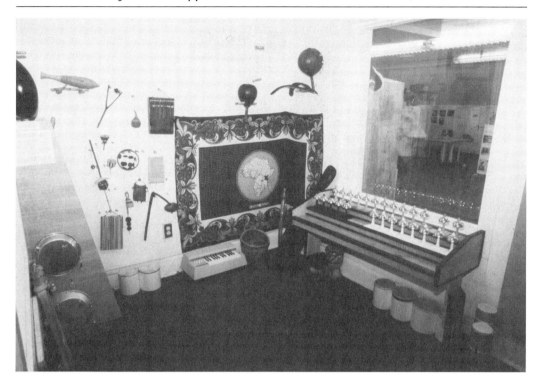

games. A new built-in light table sat on the floor with a mirror behind reaching to the low, sloped roof; it displayed a changing collection of reflective, shiny, or transparent colored objects to arrange or build—nesting boxes, round cans, or pieces of varied light baffles.

Dining Room

The Dining Room was easy. I "punched up" the white walls with tables painted in high-gloss enamel, rich aubergine for color contrast. The construction shop built shelving on two walls; on a third we hung sweeping and cleaning equipment. On the fourth the shop installed a hanging system, similar to the museum's, for easy mounting of panels. The same system was installed throughout hallways. Any doubt about the need for a dedicated Dining Room vanished when it immediately filled with parties, feasts, and large-scale work.

Bathrooms

Redesigning the bathrooms was a detailed process. At IKEA I found attractive small modular wooden drawers, to store personal bathroom items, and smart fabrics—a rich turquoise and handsome check of turquoise, burnt orange, and indigo. In the fall the teachers found a parent who could sew. She bordered the turquoise with the check, making curtains to replace the toilet stalls' drab white plastic ones. She also sewed covers which another parent used to upholster a new bench. The shop replaced three small sinks with one large one to accommodate water-play sculpture as in Reggio bathrooms. We also copied Reggio's idea of mirrored patterns on the walls.

Big Room

The Big Room was the most challenging because it served such different functions. I added small porcelain lamps and more homelike furniture. The teachers wanted children to view slides easily, so we installed a commercial slide stand in a dedicated area, wired so children could turn it on safely. A detailed poster of a countryside from an Italian stationer's, mounted in a corner of the train area at floor level, was reflected and extended by a mirror, giving the space depth and reality.

I redesigned the housekeeping area, making the appliances look real by using actual parts—small sink, faucet, burners—around which the shop built an eat-in kitchen with stove, sink, refrigerator, countertop, and cupboards. It was child-sized, but looked real because I included stainless steel, ceramics, laminates, plexiglass, and enamel in the designs. IKEA stores and Italian street markets yielded charming kitchen utensils or dining items.

I didn't sleep much that summer, consumed by design and construction details, fearing the teachers might be displeased. After all, I was redesigning their environment. I met them in September with trepidation. To my relief, they loved it, gleefully exploring each area! A drawback was their fear of changing anything, considering it my space. It took time for them to begin using the environment for their own ideas. If I could do it again, I would close the school and engage them in the design-build process. But, looking back, we were impatient to begin; a collaborative design process might have consumed a year, or distracted the teachers from their main job—being with the children and orchestrating the educational program.

TAKING STOCK

In the months leading to the rebuilding at the end of school year 1991–92, we had studied the Reggio Approach, cleaned up the environment, and haltingly attempted some Reggio practices. But even rebuilt, the space was undeveloped compared to Reggio environments, and items on shelves were still not purposeful in the Reggio sense. Classroom routines were arbitrary, unresponsive to the rhythm of a human community with its daily moods and changes. Families, while pleased, were mainly uninvolved. The teachers' focus was more on what they were doing than on the children's responses. Our one easy change had been expanding the collections in the block and train areas. Our strongest assets that spring of 1992 were Book Sharing, the teachers' courage, and the children's spirit.

Book Sharing

The best practice instituted that tumultuous year—when there were three successive directors—was Book Sharing. Teachers sent a book home with each child every night, asking families to read it together and return it the next morning. It required time—lugging books from the public library, personalizing a ziplock bag for each child, selecting books with the children, checking 36 books in and out daily.

Book Sharing generated spirited negotiations among the children about who would take which book and between children and parents, who developed favorites. Parents' responses on a questionnaire indicated the books were read, one said sometimes two or three times. Another enjoyed the fact that she and her child were learning together. Another was pleased that her daughter became responsible, reading to her brothers. Another said the more she read, the more her son wanted to read. One asked when we would get new books since they had read them all two or three times! The staff was certain it was worth the effort, and Book Sharing continued as an important daily activity.

Courageous Teachers

Sonya Shoptaugh was motivated to work with economically deprived children, was extremely empathetic, and was an excellent listener. She had a passion for working with children. She was also an accomplished photographer, developing the black-and-white portraits of the children and providing many of the school's other photographs. An early childhood education major, she was eager to try new ideas in this her first job.

Wendy Baldwin was in search of better ways to help children learn. She brought the wisdom of experience. Older by almost a generation, her 20 years in traditional preschools had frustrated her, finally driving her out. She loved what we were attempting, and her calm nature helped us all feel centered, particularly the families, who found her serenity comforting and grandmotherly.

Jennifer Azzariti was a talented artist, her medium being paper. She had a designer's eye in shaping panels and a craftsperson's agility with tools. Once she understood the role of the Studio and studio teacher, she excelled in engaging children in new challenges and introducing materials throughout the school. She had an artist's striving for perfection and an innate sense of how to elicit children's best performance.

Genet Astatke was very young, shy, and retiring. She blossomed under circumstances that made her voice equal, her perceptions valued. She developed the courage to manage the class, then hold conversations, then embark on projects. Her growth was an example of the Reggio practice of putting a new teacher alongside an experienced one so she can be shaped by the environment and the ethic.

The four shared a willingness to jump with no safety net. Undaunted by the early chaos and motivated by the new vision, all possessed a quality of mind that made them willing to undergo the hardships in trying something new. These teachers had courage.

Spirited Children

At year-end 1993 Wendy said, "I think the best thing about these students is that they have a lot of love to give, love and hugs and kisses all day long. And they are very bright; they are able to learn anything you put in front of them." Sonya added, "I think the sense of wonder is the most inspiring thing; these kids are so excited about the smallest things." Jennifer remarked, "The toughest thing is you wish you could take away all their pain. If I could change anything, I would give them a safe environment, so they could play outside without being afraid of being shot."

The children talked about shooting, police, jail, theft, drugs, and other subjects that should not concern young children. But, even living with these circumstances daily, they were like all children: They had best friends, favorite pastimes, mischievous moments, least liked foods, fascination with animals, love for their families and teachers, and zest.

A LONG WAY TO GO

The MELC's intangible assets and newly redesigned physical space did not make us a model. We had given form to our Reggio adaptation by changing our words and remaking the environment. Nevertheless, we could not give substance. None of us knew how to engage in the focused dialogues with children that take place in Reggio, or how to explore the potential in materials or listen to and reflect on children's words and actions in the ways particular to Reggio.

Had we truly realized how much we had to learn, we would have been overwhelmed, but we were too unaware to be afraid. We had many questions. Could we

- Practice the belief that children are rich, strong, and powerful?
- Fully involve families and community?
- Work in small groups with multiple projects happening simultaneously?
- Use a studio (*atelier*) and documentation?
- Provide ongoing teacher development?

Other questions were posed by members of the high-powered Washington delegation TNLC had taken to Reggio, a largely African American group that included prominent members of Washington's early childhood establishment:

- How do you engage in dialogue with a community in a way that validates the community?
- How do you really listen and remember?
- How do you figure out what it means so you know what the next steps are?

These big questions lay at the heart of what we had to learn.

If Reggio teachers appear casual, their work effortless, it is because their practices have emerged gradually. They are not struggling with new approaches; their ways have been diligently recorded, deeply studied, intentionally habituated over decades. Therefore, today the philosophy is fully instantiated in practice. Moreover, Reggio teachers are extremely articulate about their ideas, enabling experienced teachers to help new ones effectively. Not one of us, however, was experienced in the Reggio Approach.

How were we to begin? How to build a bridge from inner-city Washington to schools in a small town thousands of miles away? How to adapt what they had accomplished over decades?

As we began, several characteristics of the Reggio approach struck us as critical: the ultimate attention paid to the environment's every detail; the huge effort to analyze what children say and do; the partnership among teachers; *all* adults' equal engagement with the children; the sensitivity to the difference between doing things for children and letting them do things themselves. Because the MELC teachers could envision themselves doing these things, those seemingly small steps were where they started.

CHAPTER 4

First Steps

Conversation gives children a sense of their own agency, of possibilities, an understanding that they are expected to interact and negotiate with others.

Jerome Bruner

The MELC teachers made four commitments in September 1992: record children's conversations, begin to explore materials, keep time flexible, and start to do projects. In this chapter, I describe how they honored these commitments. They "accomplished something remarkable because they didn't know they couldn't," a phenomenon that management guru Warren Bennis calls the *beginner's mind* (Bennis & Biederman, 1997, p. 95).

Jennifer would be in the Studio using materials with small groups. Sonya and Wendy would work with small groups everywhere else. Two aides would be classroom managers, engaging uninvolved children. The teachers were eager to resume, inspired by how different we were trying to be. Each was dedicated to the children, amazed at their resilience, buoyed by their joy despite overwhelming obstacles. Others might have been intimidated, but these teachers' resolve strengthened as they confronted difficulties. They found the challenges motivating.

LEARNING TO RECORD

It is an enormous effort to record children's conversations. The most effective strategy involves placing a tape recorder close enough to a group to pick up their words, and transcribing the tapes that day or night. Then, one meets with one's colleagues soon after to study the transcriptions because timing—presenting the children with their own thoughts while they still remember—is so important.

Techniques

Holding conversations with young children requires technique and focus. The teacher does not always understand what the child says, nor does the child understand the teacher. Like playing ball with a baby who has to learn the process of back and forth, of rolling the ball in a particular direction, it is not easy for a teacher to keep a conversation focused. Nor is it easy to extract meaning from children's words. Collaboration with colleagues is vital because varied viewpoints result in more accurate interpretations. What really interests the children? How can we use their words to capture and expand these interests? Studying conversations is time-consuming and exacting.

The children's experiences also have to be documented. This involves making the large panels of words and photos that tell the story of an activity and help children maintain their interest. The MELC teachers had seen many slides of Reggio documentation, but could not grasp its purpose or how it was produced. They did not realize that the most critical decisions are which words, photos, examples of children's work, or objects to put on a panel. Then these must be logically laid out and the panel itself thoughtfully installed. Finally, for the experience to be the catalyst for an activity, teachers and children must revisit the panel. Thus documentation is essential to relate what happened and provide the stimulus to continue. When completed, a panel is a link to past projects and a bridge to future ones. As such, panels are a powerful impetus to children's engaging in Reggio-type projects. Slides had made the teachers curious about how panels were created and why there were so many, but, as they began to adapt Reggio practices, they had no inkling of the panels' complex role.

Focusing

The first conversations in school year 1992–93 were unfocused and random. For example, a recording on day one captured wandering comments: how to cook string beans; Derrick's mother bringing his sister to school tomorrow; where Sonya lived; Disneyland; trips to the park with mommy; the color of Kool-Aid. Unsure what to record, the teachers recorded too much—conversations that took place all over the school with no continuity from one to another. There were recordings of conversations between teachers and children about behavior, about techniques for using materials, about putting things away when one is finished.

In time, the teachers began to listen for *repeated* words or ideas, which helped them tease a strand out of the tangled skeins of words. They analyzed their recordings together; if different teachers had recorded similar words, it might suggest a child's real interests. If quoting a child's own words back to him rekindled his interest, bingo! If the teacher reported this to her colleagues, and if they tried and it worked—if it happened again—a focus began. Once they had a focus, they could record what was related from one day or week to the next, and begin to see where ideas might lead. When they discussed these ideas—which they had carefully harvested—with the children, and found that it did extend their interest, it suggested the direction for a project. And if the teachers asked, "What should we do next?" and the children responded enthusiastically, they were off!

EXPLORING MATERIALS

Because adults are facile at making nuanced movements, they overlook their complexity and how much a young child must learn to perform acts that seem simple, like turning a doorknob or folding paper. Introductions to materials have no goal other than to learn how materials feel in one's hands, what tools do to them, how they behave when one rolls, tears, crumples, or makes any of a hand's thousands of movements. Such exploration educates the hand.

Using Paper

In the week of September 21, Jennifer asked four children—Alonzo (4 years-1 month), Latricia (4-10), Tamika (4-9), and Tiara (4-0)—how they could change a piece of paper, and recorded the conversation below. Even at the beginning, Jennifer's innate feeling for using materials with young children is evident. She picks up on what Tamika makes, is unconcerned if a child chooses not to do something, or leaves the Studio, as Alonzo does. At first, Jennifer focused on the act of altering while the children focused on making something familiar, which they named. By the end of the session the activity transformed from *altering*—crumple, tear—to *making*—airplane, bus. Jennifer flowed easily with the change, following the children's lead.

Jennifer: Today we're going to do some things with paper. Who can tell me how we can change paper into something else?
Tamika: We can make an airplane.
Jennifer: That's *folding*. Everyone, try and fold one corner. Okay. How else can we make it look different?
Tamika: I made a little bus.
Jennifer: We can *crumple*—everyone, try to crumple a piece.
Tiara: I'm not gonna do mine.
[Tiara didn't want to tear, crumple, make holes, or in any way alter her paper.]
Latricia: A big ball.
[Jennifer folded the paper, fanlike.]
Latricia: [folding her paper] A bench, a basketball court.
Tamika: A swimming thing.

Alonzo left the Studio. Jennifer noted that he lacked interest and had weak fine motor skills. She planned to give him more cutting and a lesson on how to use scissors. Realizing that the children were interested in things, she changed her questioning.

Jennifer: Who can think of what we can do with all the paper?
Tiara: Build a house.
Jennifer: What will we need to put the house together?
Latricia: Glue.

Everyone went to get glue. With the children now making things, Jennifer introduced a different material, markers, and asked, "Can you *draw* a picture of a house?" She noted that Latricia's house had three sides. They agreed to build that house and glue three walls.

Jennifer: What will keep the rain from coming in?
Tiara: [emphatically] A top!
Jennifer: [suggesting they look at roofs from the window] What colors are they?

Tamika: White.
Tiara: Black. Flat. Big.

Jennifer revived their interest the next day by taking a walk to look at houses and roofs. She cautioned the children to look carefully for what they had forgotten on their houses. Amidst their talk, Latricia and Tamika both said, "I want to look at the trains," something that would turn into a first project.

Rolling Clay

On October 7, Jennifer began working with clay, teaching two children to roll, cut, and make shapes. She demonstrated. She encouraged them to teach each other. She limited the number of tools to ensure they grappled with the issue of sharing. She didn't give in to the younger child's impatience to handle the material before he was shown how. She herself made something, stretching their understanding of the material and techniques. These are marks of a mature teacher; yet, Jennifer had neither taught nor studied education or psychology. She had perused some craft books for ideas, but rejected most. However, as an artist, she knew materials well. Also, she connected with children in a no-nonsense way, making her expectations clear, no apology in her tone, no surplus words. This came naturally, along with her genuine appreciation for young children's ability, which they felt and in turn responded to with a serious effort (see Figure 4.1).

Working with Jameana (4-10) and Derrick (4-8), Jennifer first demonstrated how to roll clay with a rolling pin, then when Jameana tried, instructed her carefully,

FIGURE 4.1. Working in clay with Jennifer in the studio.

"Use two hands to turn it over, go over the edge [with the rolling pin], cover the whole piece. Try to get it a little thinner."

When Derrick demanded a turn, Jameana imitated Jennifer: "You can't cut it yet. You do like this." Throwing a slab on the table: "We're gonna make a lot of noise!" Repeating Jennifer's words, "Are you looking, Derrick?"

Jennifer, showing Derrick how to cut with a knife: "We only have one. You'll have to share."

The MELC children were learning how to turn a hunk of clay into a slab. Their work was what you'd expect from four-year-olds beginning to use clay. In Reggio four-year-olds experienced in using clay were making lifelike figures.

Contrast: Diana School

I returned to Reggio in March 1993 and visited the same class at Diana School, where I had observed the flow and the amazing constructions in sand and blocks. On this visit I saw a potent illustration of several key practices: work in small groups, the *atelierista*'s role, use of time as a resource, and provocative use of material.

I took notes on one particular group, four four-year-olds, sitting at a square table, one to a side. They remained there, engrossed with a big challenge, until lunch. *Atelierista* Vea Vecchi came and went, focusing on their construction. Vea had an uncanny skill for facilitating children's exploration of materials—wire, paper, paint. Her particular interest in clay was evident in the plethora of children's sculpture in the *atelier*, not made from plasticine or play dough, but from the rich low-fire gray clay that sculptors use. The school obviously had a kiln and took the children's efforts seriously, which the children understood.

Four good-sized hunks of clay, each as large as a loaf of bread, sat one on each side of the table along with tools to shape clay. There were also stands in case figures required support. Each child had a heavy board on which to work. They had been sculpting horses and riders. The current problem was to make each rider sit on a horse. The clay was pliable so there were many possibilities for integrating the figures, but also much danger. It is a big problem to keep a horse from collapsing under a rider's weight, and simultaneously make a rider sit up straight.

Francesca and Pier had completed their horses and were making riders. Tomas and Fabio had each made a horse of sorts. "Thicker here," said Tomas, adding a hunk of clay between his horse's two hind legs, making its rear more like a tree stump. Fabio had his own problems. His horse stood, but he could not imagine how to seat the rider. Realizing he needed more stability, he pushed the horse's back almost onto the table, and commented, "It's better like this."

Vea watched the progress, knowing what experiences these children had in using clay and familiar with the experiences of many others over long years. As a sculptor herself, she knew clay's potential; and from years of observing children, she knew their capacity to solve big challenges.

"What have we, Tomas?" asked Vea, looking at his tree stump. She left the room, returning shortly with more wooden support pieces. Tomas took one, wrinkled his face, removed the offending hunk of clay, reworked the legs to their original shape, and quickly shoved a support under the belly. "Ah!" exclaimed Vea with pleasure. "Now the horse stands like a horse."

Fabio protested: "But horses do not have wood underneath." "Mine does," said Tomas, pleased with the shapely hind legs and proud his horse was standing. Fabio, unsure about the wood, turned to Vea. "Yes," she nodded encouragingly, "the wood is all right." Still not convinced, Fabio pounded his animal's back. After some minutes it was spread so flat the horse shape was barely recognizable. "And, Fabio," Vea asked, "how will such a horse hold a rider?"

Fabio pondered his work, slowly reconfiguring it, until his horse stood well—with wood support. But the problem of mounting the rider remained. Meanwhile Francesca and Pier were still shaping their riders, not yet ready to seat them on horses, which were, for the present, on shelves across the room, draped with a damp cloth.

By morning's end, Tomas had gone back and forth from shapely to stumpy legs, settling at last for rather stumpy legs with wood supports, but a horse that would support a rider. Fabio had solved his problem by incorporating wood supports for both horse and rider. Pier achieved, almost from the start, an upright rider on a horse that stood with no support. Francesca's horse also supported its rider, but the rider flopped over like a rag doll and, as lunchtime arrived, refused to sit upright. Vea had encouraged, questioned, and provided materials, some requested by the children, some suggested by her. And the children, with the *atelierista*'s off-and-on presence, had compared, copied, cajoled, and consoled one another. Deeply absorbed in the same difficult problem, they were working out solutions, encouraged by the *atelierista*'s knowledge and one another's own troubles and triumphs.

The contrast between the four-year-olds in Reggio and the MELC shows what is possible when teachers believe in young children's competence to use sophisticated materials for solving challenging problems and when, by age 4, the children have already worked this way for several years.

KEEPING TIME FLEXIBLE

At the MELC the flow of the day remained essentially the same as before we began to adapt the Reggio Approach. We had always been flexible in the use of time.

Children arrived between 8:30 and 9:00, had breakfast, which could last beyond 9:30, then joined a full-group meeting which might last half an hour, mainly in discussion. Teachers listened to the children, looked at what some brought from home, admired what others had done in school yesterday. Children who had taken a walk might show what they collected. As the meeting ended, teachers asked children what they wanted to do, encouraging them to think hard before deciding. Some mentioned whom they wanted to be with rather than an activity, and the teachers encouraged these small groups to form.

After morning meeting, children followed their initial choice or pursued other choices until lunchtime at noon. After lunch most napped until 2:00, and after nap again chose what they wanted to do. Toward 4:00 everyone wound down, put things away, or protected work under way. At 4:00 the children went home. Sonya described the schedule as "loose."

Big blocks of time were at the children's disposal. Over its entire 9 years, the school was never lesson plan driven. Breakfast, morning meeting, lunch, and nap provided an outline, the only resemblance to a schedule. Sonya said, "We do not interrupt the children when they are working. Not disturbing their concentration is of prime importance" (MELC Day, 1994).

By spring of school year 1992–93, Sonya could say:

> Wendy and I often pull small groups together to work on different projects. I have a photography group [and] another working on a cat project. We may work in groups or one-on-one. Some kids choose to go into the Studio, some the Lab, so there [are] small groups working all around the school. We have a Music Room, the Water Hole, essentially the bathroom turned into water play. There's the Communication area, which is where children write messages to each other and put them in their personal mailboxes; the Lab is popular. [In the Communication Center] we have laptop computers so the children can do word processing and type notes to each other. In the Lab we have graphic design and games. Sometimes teachers take groups into the Dining Room for projects requiring more space or a quieter atmosphere.

Sonya's description reveals the teachers' success at helping children develop self-discipline, the factor that made all else possible. Now everyone could spread throughout many rooms, a major problem only a year earlier. Inspired by minimal exposure to Reggio ideas, the teachers had made more activities available, and were consciously trying to work in small groups. While the flow of time had barely changed, how the teachers used the time was changing. Activities were becoming connected across increasingly longer periods, days then weeks, and as a result were more complex. Teachers were making better use of the environment, expanding the range of materials, and beginning to notice their potential.

STARTING TO DO PROJECTS

In October, Sonya and Wendy honed in on topics that they heard repeatedly in the children's conversations. These became the first projects. Even at the beginning, the teachers recognized the importance of being attuned to children's interests. Sonya did a project on trains and Wendy did one on Coco, both subjects the teachers heard in the children's conversation. They followed through with the same children, accepted a child's dropping out or a new child's joining the group, and began to establish the kind of collaboration between teacher and group that is a hallmark of project work.

The Train Project

The school's west windows faced the railroad tracks; from them children could see Union Station, one long walking-distance block away. Its trains were part of the MELC's life, the rooms reverberating with trains' whistles and conductors' calls. Union Station, magnificently renovated in the 1980s, was almost as powerful an attraction as the trains themselves, a grand architecture with great arched ceilings, marble floors, winding stairways, long vistas, and many shops. One shop was dedicated to trains, its huge model train setup a wonderland. Teachers enriched the school's train area by purchasing postcards, a train-sounding whistle, a tape of train sounds, and other props.

The Project Starts–Thursday, October 22. Sonya observed which children were especially interested in the real trains and the toy set in the Big Room. When she initiated a conversation, it took very little to make thoughts flow. She asked only two questions. The first, "What would you like to know about trains?" generated the following responses:

Latricia (4-11): Why do the trains need to put people on them? Do they need to
    go to work or something?
Tiara (4-1): Do they go to stores to get a necklace? [Then, imagining this] "Stop!
    Somebody off! Somebody to a store to get a necklace!"
Latricia: Do they have something to eat on it? Lunch? Or breakfast? Tissues and
    a trash can?

Sonya's second question was, "How can we find out?" These two questions are powerful and universally applicable. The first taps the wealth of experiences even very young children have already accumulated. The second stretches them to make connections from one particular bit of information to their other ideas, which adults cannot intuit.

Derrick (4-9) Joins–Friday, October 23. Sonya, observing Derrick's fascination with the toy trains, the train tracks, and the sounds, asked, "What do you want to know about trains?"

Derrick: [very excited]: I want to know about *people* in the trains! Umm, the
    people, umm . . . drivin' the trains. About when the people say . . . when they
    wave to you. When the man pull the thing and the smoke come out.
Sonya: Is there anything else you would like to know?
Derrick: When the . . . when the . . . people [sounds like "bad"] the trains and
    then it make noise.
Sonya: [unsure what Derrick said, but continuing to question] When they *what*
    the trains?
Derrick: When he beeps it.
Sonya: How do you think we can find out about these things?
Derrick: We can go there tomorrow and then we could talk to them.

First Visit–Still Friday, October 23. Because the MELC staff was organized for teachers to work in small groups, Sonya could capitalize on Derrick's interest in the most powerful way: Immediately after their conversation, the two went to Union Station.

Sonya: What do you see?
Derrick: I see *trains!* I see *people!*
Stationmaster: There are doors at the end of each car where you get in. Would
    you like to stick your head in and see?

When they returned to school, Sonya asked Derrick how he could find out more about trains. He answered, "I could make one." To aid his drawing, Derrick used postcards they had just purchased and the oversized book—with photos that would please any train buff—from the MELC's train area. Sonya asked Derrick to compare the postcards and photos to his drawing, to notice details like wheels, doors, steps, and the trains' names. Even in this first project, Sonya recognized not only the driving force of a child's interest, but also the importance of scaffolding, which she did by questioning, using photos, books, and the trains themselves.

Broadening the Discussion–Wednesday, October 28. There were more points of view and questions when Donnell (4-11) joined the group the following Wednesday. Sonya asked Derrick to tell everyone what he had seen.

Derrick: I saw the people, and the man. . . . They show us how to get out. You got to stick your head down when the people come out. Then he pushed the button, then you gotta come out.
Latricia: When they push in the button, how do they step outside?
Derrick: They step on the white thing when you come out.
Latricia: They step on *rocks*?
Derrick: No! No! They step on the thing when they see something with the . . . with the *step* thing, that thing when you step on you gotta . . . you gotta put your head down and then, when you don't hurt yourself, you go to pick some cards out, bring them back to school, leave them here.
Latricia: [puzzled] You can't put your head down . . .
Derrick: [shaking his head yes] Uh huh.
Latricia: [emphatic] It's a *big* door!
Derrick: You've *got* to put your head down.
Latricia: I ain't puttin' my head down.
Derrick: You do, 'cuz you got . . . He said, "Put your head down all the time that you go down that way."

Derrick clearly remembered something he can't explain, but the other children didn't understand this business of putting your head down.

Latricia: When are we going on the trains, Sonya?
Sonya: How about Friday?
[A jumble of excited "Yes's" and "No's," which Sonya untangled]
Sonya: You want to go *today*?
All: Yes!
Sonya: Okay. Let's make a list of questions.

Going around the group, Sonya asked each in turn, "What would you like to know about trains?" The children's own questions provided the focus for the visit.

Donnell: How you get off.
Derrick: I wanna know how do the trains go ride on the tracks and stop. . . . And when the smoke come out . . . then it make noise and say "Boop, Boop."

Sonya: I don't know if they have smoke. Do you ever see the trains over there giving off smoke?

All: Yeah!

Latricia: [very excited] Wait! Wait! Wait! Wait! They have black dirt all over . . .

Derrick: [interrupting emphatically] No! . . . No, it's not! It's clean!

Sonya: We need . . . to see if the trains have steam coming out of them, because I don't know. . . . That's my question.

Tiara: I want to make a picture of the trains.

Latricia: Can you live in the train?

Sonya: Good question! We can draw the trains after we get back so make sure you look and make sure you *see*!

Second Trip–Still Wednesday, October 28. Spirits were high as Sonya and four children left for Union Station. Sonya had arranged to have the group meet a station attendant that very day. Ms. Mickle told them not to be bashful.

Latricia asked, "Do they have something to eat on the train?" Ms. Mickle explained about short trips, long trips, and the different kinds of food.

Next, Derrick asked, "How do the smoke come out?" Ms. Mickle pointed out the wires, explaining the difference between electric and diesel power.

Then Tiara aked, "How do you get out?" And Ms. Mickle answered, "Well, they got doors. . . . Maybe we can go on one and see." Latricia, Tiara, and Derrick boarded the train with Ms. Mickle. Sonya stayed behind with Donnell, who was afraid.

When the three returned, Sonya asked them to tell Donnell what they saw.

Derrick: We saw chairs, no people on 'em. We was sittin' down on it and . . . it was real soft, readin' our books.

Sonya: [clarifying what was a great confusion] Did you have to put your heads down?

All the children shook their heads from side to side. Sonya, emphasizing their new understanding, said, "Nope!"

The teachers were learning to use children's statements about what they'd done as a way to spread ideas to other children and to use children's own words as the most effective way to pique their memory and keep their interests alive: "Do you remember . . . ?" "Yesterday you said that . . ." Careful listening tells children that teachers respect them and encourages children to value their own ideas. It also maintains their focus. It does not necessarily reveal what children mean. Even now, after analyzing Derrick's remarks to relate this story, I am not sure what he was talking about when he said you had to "put your head down." At this stage, their first real project, the MELC teachers and children have had little practice at extracting meaning from conversation. As the teachers refined their techniques, they began to realize that their notes and recordings were valuable sources for the children's words, and began to study them to find just the right words. They also began to carry clipboards with drawing paper so children could draw with details directly in front of them. In these ways they exploited experiences in order to foster projects.

Thinking About What We've Seen–Even Later Wednesday, October 28. Back at school after the visit, Latricia and Donnell decided to paint pictures of trains, Derrick and Tiara to draw. Over the following days, Sonya recorded the children's explanations of their drawings. Each had a different theory of what makes trains run.

Drawing Train Sounds–Friday, November 6. A week later Sonya told the group she had purchased a tape of train sounds because Derrick said, "The train is singing!" Excited, the children helped move the tables in the Dining Room and unroll large sheets of paper on the floor to draw train sounds.

First the children listened with their eyes closed, then Sonya handed out black charcoal for them to draw as they listened to the tape again. The children listened intently as they drew (see Figure 4.2).

Tiara: I don't know how to draw sound.
Latricia: You just draw what you hear.

FIGURE 4.2. Train sound. (Drawing)

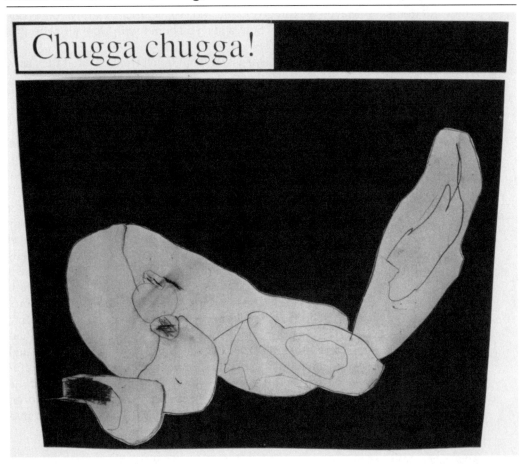

Derrick: [repeatedly exclaiming] Hoot! Hoot! That's the steam sound. Hoot!
  Hoot!
Latricia: Chugga chugga choo choo.
Tamika (who had joined the group for this activity): Choo choo.
Tiara: [drawing steadily] Chugga chugga chugga. Chugga chugga chugga . . .

Derrick and Tiara went on to something else as Donnell had, their interest
in trains sated for now. Latricia and Tamika helped Sonya spray fixative to keep
the charcoal from smudging, and hang the drawings in the Dining Room. Two
months later, the teachers rehung them in the Big Room, nearer the trains.

Reflecting. Ideas need time to gestate, especially after intense experiences.
Sonya let several days intervene after Derrick's first visit to Union Station. The following Wednesday when she engaged the children in conversation, they became
so excited they wanted to visit the trains that instant—so they went the same day.
Returning to school with images fresh in their minds, they drew. Days later, one-
on-one, Sonya recorded their theories. Over a week passed before they listened to
train sounds and drew them. The different experiences took place over a period of
3 weeks. The project succeeded because trains were part of the immediate environment and fascinated the children, because the teachers pursued their interest,
and because the school was organized—its staff, time, and space—for small-group
work.

Gradually, the teachers helped children to be more focused in their conversations, more detailed in their drawings. They asked questions like How . . . ?
Why . . . ? Can you . . . ? to elicit questions from the children. To find answers, they
encouraged the children to use the environment—objects, books, the library, family members. From the first, they realized the importance of continuing a project
with the same group, neither adding new children (although occasionally a child
might leave and a new one join) nor repeating an experience with other children.
Intuitively, they knew that every child did not need to have the *same* experience. A
distinguishing feature of Reggio practices is the belief that every child does not have
to experience everything (or anything) that another child does. Early on, the MELC
teachers trusted that all children would have experiences of equal value no matter
how experiences differed. If American policy makers could grasp only this point—
that experience does not have to be the same to be of equal value—it could create
a revolution from child care through high school.

Coco—Many Projects

Wendy noticed the children's fascination with the school's cat. Coco often
stretched out on the light table (see Figure 4.3); sometimes he pawed at the
goldfish's bowl, curled up on a soft coat in a cubby, or hovered around the Dining Room at mealtime. Wendy frequently discussed how to treat Coco: not to hold
him too tight or drop him, not to chase him or pinch his ears, not to pull his tail,
not to wake him if he was asleep, and especially not to open his eyes while he
slept.

These discussions led Wendy to ask what the children knew about cats. To
expand their knowledge, she had a small group "read" books to her. Each child

FIGURE 4.3. Coco on the light table. (Studio)

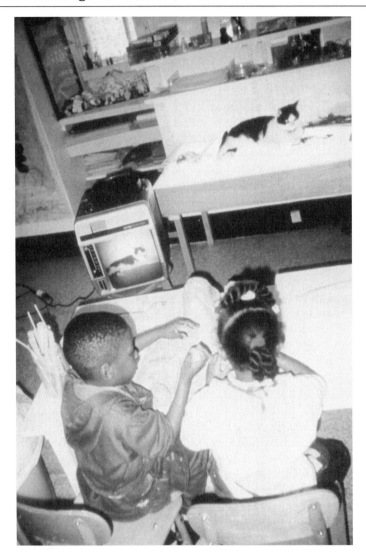

selected a book about cats from the classroom library and used the pictures to tell
Miss Wendy and the other children the story (see Figure 4.4). Eventually the interest
moved into the Studio, where Jennifer did a project comparing hand- and footprints
to Coco's paw prints. By winter, cat projects grew more complex—videotaping Coco,
taking him to the vet, drawing the trip. Later projects would be even more challenging: detailed drawings in pencil or fine-point markers; clay models; helping Coco
establish a relationship with a turtle, and reproducing the experience with varied
materials; writing about him.

Before and after each step in a project, teachers used the children's own
words and photographs to remind them what they'd asked, what they'd learned,

FIGURE 4.4. *Reading* to Miss Wendy about cats. (Book Sharing Area)

how they'd reacted. This remembering spurred a project along. So did adding more resources to the classroom—reference books, pictures, slides—and using other languages—clay, ink, paint, cardboard.

At this time, winter 1993, teachers were asking children both to engage in the give-and-take of conversation and to make comparisons, like contrasting the cat's paw prints to their own hand- and footprints. The teachers kept the children on track, rarely commenting when the children digressed, repeatedly asking the same question. It took a full week for the children to grasp what it meant to compare paws, hands, and feet, to note differences in size, to see the relation between claws and fingernails. It took months to become focused in conversation, to observe, to make comparisons. But the teachers persisted, consistently encouraging the children to contrast, question, and attend to detail; to describe it, draw it, or represent it concretely.

The Many Images of Coco. Two years later, in school year 1994–95, the teachers and 16 children explored Coco's feelings and his role in their lives, and presented the results in a book. It required many conversations and drawing sessions—some in small groups, others one-on-one—and many recordings, transcriptions, and discussions to generate the book's 62 comments and 23 drawings. The introduction says: "Every one of us has a special, unique, and complicated personality, including Coco."

The following comments taken from the book show a greatly increased capacity for focused conversation and observation. (The number in parentheses indicates if it's a child's first, second, or third year in the MELC.)

Tanya (1): Coco has four paws.
Ceola (2): He's black and white.
Ronald (2): His eyes are light green.
Glenn (2): He has a tail.
Stefan (2): Coco has soft hair.
Maulana (2): His nose is wet.
Brandi (3): Coco is a boy cat.
E. C. (1): Sometimes Coco is happy, sometimes he's mean.
Cherise (2): Coco speaks, he makes a sound—"meow meow."
Maulana: He likes to drink the colored water in the Studio.
Mary Ann (1): Coco likes to stay on the light table. He likes to sleep there.
Ronald: He likes to be scratched. . . . He likes to be rubbed. When you pet him you can feel his heart beating.
Willie (2): Coco has a special spot in the school near the climber. He eats his food there.
Robert (1): Sometimes it smells bad there; you have to hold your nose.
Mary Ann: He doesn't put water on him, he licks himself. That's how they take baths.
Eric (3): When Coco wants to sleep, he closes his eyes.
Willie: He likes to sit on the black chair.
Maulana: The black chair is by the Storeroom. He goes there because that's the quiet room. He doesn't like to hear loud noise.
Tamika (2): He was sleeping on the chair and he was tired from the kids playing with him all day.

The children commented on everything—Coco's appearance, his feelings, where he sleeps. The seemingly endless digressions that dominated conversation 2 years earlier have fallen away. Conversations come easily because now the teachers know how to plan for them, how to use their collective observations to choose topics, how to recognize which comments are most likely to move the conversation ahead. The children have had experience noticing details, drawing them, and following through on an idea. Their attention span is now long enough to create a 25-page book. Because they worked with the same group over 3 years, the teachers could see these changes.

Coco the Cat. In January 1993 Tyresha (5-9) joined Donnell (5-3), LaShay (5-4), and Renée (4-8) on the cat project. Supported by the museum's video department, teachers asked if the children wanted to make a video about Coco. The children learned to load tape, focus the camera, point, shoot, and understand the essence of editing—selecting what you want to show and sequencing it. They learned to use complicated equipment in which the effect of turning a knob or pushing a button is not readily apparent. The result was a 5½-minute video. It was a big hit with the other children and teachers. The museum's and Options School's staff liked it. So did educators who saw it at the 1993 NAEYC annual meeting.

The following year the *Washington Times* reviewed short films by children that were included in the annual Environmental Film Festival. The article was illustrated with two photos of three MELC children using a video camera. It reported:

> In *Coco the Cat* a group of 4- and 5-year-olds simply play with, observe, and enjoy a cute cat. . . . 4-year-old Renée Brown and friends simply turned their camera on their cat, Coco, with a resulting straightforward look at a cat from the kids' perspective. (Neufeld, 1994, p. B1)

BEGINNINGS

In school year 1992–93 the teachers' growth was reflected in an environment that was beginning to blossom. In a single year they went from tentative projects to projects actually lasting weeks. The first were less than 30 minutes, like making clay balls and worms, to as long as 2 consecutive days, like collecting leaves one day and using them for a collage the next. Some were small provocations from the teachers, like putting gels on a window for the color to reflect on an opposite wall or on the floor, then watching to see children's reactions. Gradually, projects expanded to several days, like making self-portraits from Mylar and found objects, or planning a holiday feast, including decorating, making gifts for their families, and preparing the food. By April, projects lasted weeks, like Alphotography (see Chapter 9) or videotaping Coco. In spring a project on the environment—using children's words, drawings, or collage to describe everything in the school—lasted 3 months.

The increase in projects' length and complexity reflected the teachers' growth, which resulted from many factors: their individual natures and competencies; their relief that, even after the third director had left, they could maintain discipline. They were inspired by the Reggio Approach and satisfied at finally having a direction for the school. They felt part of cutting-edge change, which they knew the Reggio approach represents. They were pleased by other educators' enthusiastic responses. Above all, the children's growth and families' beginning involvement motivated the teachers to reflect on what they were doing, to tease out what accounted for the changes, and do more of the same. Circumstances that were particular to the MELC also contributed to their growth—the school's location in a city rich with stimulation, some visible from the school's windows; the ratio of 36 children to five staff, which fostered small-group work. Every place is special in its own ways, however, and any class with two adults—often a state requirement—can be organized to support small-group work.

Two big changes were essential to begin work in small groups. One was elevating the aide's role, dropping the title *aide*, calling everyone *teacher*, and giving everyone's observations equal weight. This demanded that everyone become a skilled listener and redefined everyone's role. The second change was letting go of any guilt the teachers may have felt about focusing on a particular group of children, learning to trust that experiences, even if vastly different, were equally valuable in a child's development. These were not changes that could be observed during a visit. But, as the first Reggio-inspired year ended, visitors could observe the complexity of the space, the many materials, the mass of children's work displayed everywhere, and the high-level thinking represented in that work. And visitors were impressed.

The MELC teachers had two daunting tasks: changing fundamental beliefs and doing so quickly, at most in 2 to 3 years, not over the decades in which Reggio practices had evolved. They wanted to change, and the new vision required them to have faith in children's strength, which meant stifling their instinct to "teach" and relying instead on their responses to children's actions, in effect, throwing away lesson plans. They had to reorganize themselves to support small-group work. They had to use feedback from their own observations. They felt almost feisty and succeeded because they were superb people. Outsiders affirmed their success. I praised every tiny step. I loved their attempts, the mere fact that they *were* attempting.

Beginnings are hard to capture, especially in human development. The steps are neither predictable, as in moviemaking, nor quantified, as in building a house. Processes through which humans develop cannot be observed. It would require endless hours of images to see the millions of movements culminating in a baby's first step or leading to a child's first penciled letter.

Harvard professor Roger Brown, father of developmental psycholinguistics, laid the groundwork to understand the sequence of acquiring language. To describe the beginnings of the process, Brown and his students analyzed countless hours of recordings. After 18 months, the process became too complicated to follow:

> The children's rate of development and their linguistic sophistication far outran the ability of Brown and . . . [his] students . . . to analyze and understand all that was happening. Brown said the movement was "more like a sheet of lava than an arrow . . . [and called it] "cumulative complexity." . . . "Before children can acquire the plural they must understand number, and before they can acquire the past tense they must understand earlierness. . . . Brown did not go beyond [the early stages] because he could no longer find the same regularities in the later stages. . . . [It] became too complex. (DeCuevas, 1990, pp. 65–66)

The MELC had two simultaneous, highly complex beginnings: the teachers' beginning to use an extremely sophisticated set of integrated theories and practices; and the children's continuing the process, which begins at conception, of laying foundations for their mental, physical, and social being. One day a project may be barely recognizable, or a conversation may ramble, bordering on incoherent. Several months later all the remarks cohere, or a comprehensive project is documented. But the change has not occurred step-by-step and cannot be easily explained or readily duplicated.

Imagine a workman taking shovelfuls of sand from a pile. One day, as he removes a shovelful, the pile collapses. He did not expect this, and even if he had, there was no way to predict which shovelful would undermine the structure. Expressed differently, it requires a critical mass of sand to make a pile; below critical mass there is no pile. Tom Sayre, a young artist fascinated by such phenomena, shot over a hundred photographs of collapsing wooden fences. Some showed a standing fence, some a fallen heap of boards; most interesting were the ones where the form was still recognizable but hovered on collapse, the moment between fence and not fence, that split second before the loss of critical mass, the exquisite tension between *is* and *is not*.

Human formation involves the same exquisite tensions, but infinitely more complex. In human development one can neither set a timetable on which to provide experiences nor foresee which experiences will culminate in the critical mass essential to a specific behavior. The process of accumulating experience is so subtle, so intricate, that whether or when something recognizable will emerge is unpredictable. This chapter has attempted to describe a few experiences in the emergence of Reggio practices in the MELC, the beginning steps of its teachers and children.

CHAPTER 5

Straight-Talking Guidance

The adults' difficulty is to initiate and nurture situations that stimulate . . . [a] learning process where conflict and negotiation . . . [are] the driving forces for growth.

Carlina Rinaldi

By winter of school year 1992–93, activities began to feel purposeful. Children and teachers engaged in projects that teachers portrayed in documentation. Yet their frustration was mounting. Sonya and Wendy felt there must be more. Jennifer felt isolated from the others, unsure how her work in the Studio and theirs connected. They did not know how to go deeper. I was not able to guide them; the strain was showing. We needed help.

SEEKING ANSWERS IN REGGIO

On February 23, 1993, I returned to Reggio with two purposes. First, I would continue planning the Reggio Emilia Symposium, a national conference that TNLC was hosting in keeping with its mission of exploring and promoting cutting-edge ideas: We wanted to expose new audiences, including our own staff, to the Reggio Approach. The second purpose was to seek answers to the teachers' many questions. I elicited advice from Tiziana Filippini and Carlina Rinaldi, and observed in the 4-year-olds' classroom at Diana School.

Pedagogista Tiziana Filippini listened to my long list of questions: How do you decide what projects to do? How do you select children for particular projects? What if just one child is interested? How do you add children to projects? How long do projects last anyway? She was polite until I asked, "If a child loses interest mid-project, do you let that child leave?" Her response was resounding: "Think about what *you* have done! How did *you* offer? Did *you* lose interest?" Then she added, a less ambiguous response, "Another child can join if he's not jumping every which way."

Some questions reflected behavioral difficulties we still had: How do you prevent children's fighting over who does what with whom? How do you foster cooperation rather than competition? Do children ever have difficulty focusing with no strong interest emerging? Tiziana said children have varying *thicknesses* of concentration. A teacher truly attentive to the child's interest can engage her more easily. If the child is having trouble concentrating, perhaps the teacher should value her interests more.

Some questions were about organization: How do you dismiss morning meeting? How do you decide what will happen on a particular day? Tiziana answered in questions: What came before? Where is each child? Always consider how the project was prepared, defined, whether it was clear. She gave an example: A teacher had made a construction to explore shadows. The children had experienced shadows. But, as the project evolved, shadows did not emerge as its focus. Considering how they should have proposed the project, they concluded they should have seduced the children with something spectacular, or had a warm-up period, 10 minutes, a day, or 3 days playing with gesture. "Clarify the theory, then the strategy will follow."

What, Tiziana asked, were the children's own words, their images, their theories? Reggio teachers use children's ideas as the spur to continue. I must have looked incredulous because she added, "They really do!"

I knew the answers I conveyed wouldn't satisfy the teachers. In fact, to every question they heard one answer: It depends! Reggio children's competence and their teachers' approaches still seemed vastly removed.

I explained to Carlina our struggling, our seemingly endless questions, the need to go deeper. She suggested asking Amelia Gambetti to help. Retired from teaching, she was doing consulting work in the United States and finally agreed to visit the MELC. Carlina's advice added authority to the urgent pleas I had made on numerous calls from Washington to Amherst, where Amelia was consulting.

AMELIA CRITIQUES THE MELC

That school year Amelia was at the Laboratory School of the University of Massachusetts. In February, observing the teachers' frustration, I had called, pleading for help. Amelia's initial response was, "It is impossible to find time." The upcoming symposium was the catalyst: "How can we have people from throughout the United States look at the MELC when we are so unsure of what we are doing?" Aware of Reggio's huge commitment to the symposium, she conceded. She would steal a couple of days and come to Washington.

I returned from Reggio on March 2. Late on March 4, Amelia arrived. The next day, Friday, she observed from 9 to 4, everything, including lunch, nap, and dismissal. Until way past dinner, she showed Reggio slides. I took notes on everything.

Touchpoints: The Reggio Schools

Amelia began with environments: Children have a *right* to a good environment, one that encourages people to linger, is full of provocations, and reflects the different personalities of people living in the space. Materials are a big provocation, stored in the classroom so the children can see everything.

Amelia explained unfamiliar images in the slides. A mirror, curved like several S's and made from highly polished aluminum, transformed reality. Patterns on the floors provoked children to play with symbols. Objects on shelves in the mini-*atelier* that had fascinated us were collections; they created a sense of belonging, a glimpse of the teacher's life, reflecting her personality and visual sensibilities. Complex constructions of intertwining pipes in bathrooms were made by parents.

Amelia related how Reggio teachers met with parents to discuss materials, asking them to help collect and organize them. In this way parents and teachers discover more about one another. "We use parents' hands to build new relationships because materials evoke something particular to a person."

The presentation ended with a traditional Italian poem:

Uno due tre	One two three
Si resti te	If you remain yourself
Sarai re.	You will be king (powerful).

Analyzing the MELC

Saturday we gathered at 9 in the morning. First, Amelia related general impressions; then we toured the school. Until long after lunch we walked through the entire school looking at everything while Amelia critiqued it all in a running commentary on what we could do. She provided many ideas, expanding what we had begun, offering new directions. Many of her observations and suggestions follow.

Amelia's debriefing was a tour de force (see Figure 5.1) reflecting 20 years of experiences: her own formation when at age 19 she had first worked with Malaguzzi; the times he had asked her to prepare an environment or coach staff in a new school; her own classroom over the decades when Reggio practices were forming; her relationship working for years with *atelierista* Giovanni Piazza. Amelia couched her observations carefully, supporting our accomplishments, trying to fulfill our desire to go deeper. Sensing the staff's hunger, she spoke freely: "When you have had a good experience, you are more open to other situations, more flexible."

FIGURE 5.1. Amelia debriefs the MELC teachers.

Amelia began with some general suggestions: Add more to every area. Write. Let the children see you write titles for panels. Have the children write titles. Type transcribed dialogues to hang in transparent envelopes wherever the activity occurred and read them again. Noting each room's description, she said, "Add children's words as well as examples of what the children do there." Titles could be children's words: "We are doing . . . " "We are using . . . " Adding children's photos gives them a sense of belonging.

Documentation. Amelia talked at length about documentation. Whenever a project starts, we should hang an empty panel nearby as documentation in progress, explaining what we're trying to accomplish. It should contain a photo of the children and photos of work in progress.

Amelia also commented about techniques. She urged using only white backgrounds: "Putting labels on the same color paper will make children notice." She suggested, when planning to add children's work, providing drawing paper sized to fit the panel easily. Above all, children's words and black-and-white drawings should be everywhere: "Think about what presence children could have here. Their words are another point of view." Instead of saying "children's artwork," say "production," "work," or "activity of children." "Photos!" she exclaimed. "Put them *everywhere.*" For example, in the block area add photos of different constructions; leave blank space for children's words; hang things from the ceiling suggesting construction.

Documentation is not a final product but a *process.* Starting with an empty panel, which turns into a panel in progress, is saying, This is a project we are carrying on. As they plan, teachers should ask, What kind of documentation will best portray this project? Products cannot be planned, but processes can.

The teachers asked what kinds of projects to do. Amelia responded immediately: "Spring! What are you doing about spring? What are the children doing? How can you document it? Words, photos, video, drawings, paint." If images are needed, families could collect them from newspapers and magazines.

She urged us to engage children in the process of documentation, discussing with them the means they would use, the records they would make. She gave us precise words as an example:

> OK, last week we decided we would go see the flowers. What do
> you need to take? Bring something back to school to help you
> remember the trip. What will you need to carry it? Can you sketch
> when you are there? What do you need for sketching? a pencil?
> some paper? a clipboard? I think I will need your voices, the sound
> of the river, the birds, the cars, so I will take the tape recorder. Do
> we want images? Then we will need the camera.

Amelia provoked us further: "Before doing something with children, do it yourselves. Don't improvise questions to ask the children; think them up in advance. In every situation, begin by asking children their opinion and pay attention to their words."

Amelia enumerated a list of steps for creating a panel:

1. Decide where you will put panel sequences about spring field trips.
2. Start with the title on an empty panel.
3. Have children help write the titles.
4. Tell them: Here we will put the bus ticket, here photos of the field trip, here a postcard or flower, an immediate reminder of the trip.
5. Build the panel step-by-step so there is not lots of work at the end.
6. Create panels together, all of you, with the *atelierista*.
7. Invite an outsider to read the panel for clarity.

She was adamant that we talk with children about documentation before beginning and take them in small groups after it was hung to read the story to remind them of their experiences and stimulate them to continue. Ask, "Do you recognize this?" Read it with the children and reread it frequently (see Figure 5.2).

Time and Planning. Amelia addressed "dead time," emphasizing it could be teacher time. In extra times, with or without children, teachers and *atelierista* should work together in the *atelier* building the panels. She explained how the Reggio system of organization provides time aside from teaching for teachers' other work. She was emphatic: "*Use the time!* Teachers' days are not done at 5. Children are not sheets of paper. You can't forget their problems or do this job by the clock."

She suggested that we make a theme for a week, 15 days, a month, a *big* goal. Then we should divide it into small objectives, and each day do something. Frustration comes from having lots of ideas and not enough time. "Be flexible. If you plan but something else happens, immediately stop the plan; follow what happened." Such strategies deepen and broaden children's interests.

Materials. Amelia critiqued our use of materials. We did not have enough out. Children were only using materials already in an area. We should ask children playing with the trains, "Would you like to add blocks?" Or, children playing with blocks, "Would you like to add animals?" Or, children in the house, "Would you like to add seeds?" Then go get them!

Teachers should play with materials: For example, put a huge sheet of paper on the floor and walk, swim, roll on it. Or wrap a person, an object. Discover the pleasure of the material. Teachers should be taking notes of the children's words: Their impressions would help us find a way to teach them.

Amelia suggested that we put more materials on the *atelier*'s shelves, play with them ourselves, and talk with the children about them, for example in this way: "Now we have such incredible materials. Would you like to build a mobile with me to put on the ceiling? It can be fantastic; it will be so beautiful!"

Layering the Environment. Amelia told us to put arrows, about 5"× 5" from sturdy tape, on the floor to layer the environment. More materials in the block area—seashells, plastic pipe, tubes, stones, rope, strips of paper—are not a mess, but something different. It makes the familiar new, satisfying a basic human need for novelty and complexity. She urged us to jump into it, observe, try. We would learn lots watching the children. "Make it a layered environment!" she said repeatedly.

FIGURE 5.2. Following Amelia's advice, Miss Wendy revisits documentation with a group.

Mobiles should hang from the ceiling, built from different things, even origami. If you don't know how to do origami, learn it with the children, and use simple folds to make a house, a star, a sheep. Put the shapes in sequence, like a story. Mobiles require clear, thin, clean support so the hanging object is the attraction. Search the environment or find suitable materials on trips. Choose thoughtfully. Take notes and document the process.

Numbers, Letters, Symbols. Amelia suggested using numbers more, playing with concepts like classification and seriation. We should have a jar for each number and a transparent bag full of different numbers, some in strips, some written by children, some cut from newspapers. Use them as labels. Ask children to pick a number, then use the number they pick to have them do something: "Find the corks. Screw the tops on jars."

Undertake research with the children: "Where do you see numbers at home? at school?" Calendars are examples of numbers at school. Examples of measurement are bus schedules, rulers, clocks, thermometers, telephones, phone books. Ask: "What is this? How is it used? Why are there divisions? Do you know what a day is? a week? a month? an hour? a minute?" It would be a treasure hunt for measurement.

Children could collect letters of the alphabet. Ask them, "Can you cut letters? Can you cut titles?" Children are curious about these. Put each in its own jar to use in writing. Ask for parents' help; let them know their children are writing.

Use three different forms of representation—children's name, photo, and symbol—everywhere. Using these together shows them what communication is and that you can say the same thing in different ways. Arrows help children understand how symbols communicate. We began to realize that concrete arrows, abstract letters, symbols are some of the *100 languages*.

HOW TO USE THE ENVIRONMENT

Amelia underscored the relation between children and the environment—furnishings, school, museum, city—and explained how to build links everywhere, to "read the environment with the children."

Environment as a Context

In the Big Room, the Montessori map stand with the puzzle of each continent caught Amelia's attention and elicited her suggestions. Maps could help children understand their environment. Start by showing them real maps. Challenge them to draw a map. Accept every production! If one or two children seem especially interested, push them ahead. Introduce Montessori maps to a different group. Ask children what they think happens in these places, how children there live. Add photos showing children using the maps, also their words and opinions. Make them delicate and beautifully written.

Seeing the posted floor plan for an escape route, Amelia suggested showing children the words "YOU ARE HERE." Ask them: "Do you know what this is? Can you read this? Can you help me understand?" Add a label to the fire extinguisher: "What is this?" Then put up children's explanations. Children should understand everything about where they are. Washington is famous for museums. Introduce city maps, postcards, photographs.

> Washington is your *context*. It is your children's town! You are in a children's museum; but nothing says that! Have pictures, photos, maps of your museum. Discover your building and where you are in it. Add information on the museum. Visit your director's office. Interview her!

At an end-of-morning meeting summarize, having each group explain what they've done: "Show me what you did today." She was explaining the importance of children's involvement with the environment and suggesting techniques to connect them to it. Simultaneously, she was explaining how these integrate in a day's routine, how to manage the flow. We wanted the information, but it was a lot to absorb.

Organizing an Overview

We spent a long time in the Greeting Room. Amelia admired the wall full of children's large photos, but told us to add their *presence*, to include something each child had made and said alongside the photo. It would become a big mural that said: "Here we are! We like the school!" Things made by children layer the environment and enliven the adult's style.

Amelia said we should add the staff's names and photos, individual and group, with children's portraits of and comments about their teachers. Their voices could describe janitors, Frank (facilities manager), Jorgé (electrician), everyone. Then others could see the school through the children's eyes.

Since it is so unusual to have a cat in a school, she thought we should also see Coco everywhere—photographs about him, children's drawings of him, materials about other cats (see Figure 5.3). If the children have cats at home, hang their photos.

The Greeting Room should broadcast on a big panel: "We greet children. These are their activities." It is a communication problem to solve with children's words and productions. Hang transparent folders with transcriptions so children can show what they've done in their own words. For example:

Monday March 7   A group of four children:
  [names] with [teachers' names]
We were in the dramatic play area.
We are having a birthday party.
It is Tiara's birthday.

A panel with movable photos can show who's at home today and who's at school, and is another place to use each child's name, photo, and symbol and children's words, drawings, or collage. We should keep two copies of messages, posting one on the Parent Board, the other on a panel about messages. A companion panel should portray children's mailing messages. Children would need bigger paper for these messages as well as stamps, envelopes, postcards, images to cut out, and gift wrap. Copies of messages should be stored in titled boxes—To Teachers, To Ann, To Families. Children could see how messages are used: "Would you like to do a project about the Post Office? to communicate with children who are sick at home? with Amelia in Massachusetts?"

Amelia directed many comments to the Greeting Room, places of special importance in Reggio, the hub of a school's communication, the bridge between life in and out of school, the link between school and home.

FIGURE 5.3. Drawing of Coco.

Enriching Other Rooms

Seeing a panel of children's self-portraits on a wall in the Dining Room, Amelia said: "Add children's words for the title or to show the process: This is a portrait of . . . We used this technique . . . We used these materials . . ." Other photos should convey the room's personality, reflecting what happens—close-ups of a child opening a container; using a "spork"; actual jars with beans or macaroni, a basket of onions, whatever they eat; their comments on foods they prefer and why.

She gave other suggestions related to food. If one group prepares a snack, invite another group to eat it. Document it. Interview the people who bring the food, working out questions beforehand with the children. Everything is a process with children:

We are going to characterize this room. Can you help me? How will we interview this person? With a tape recorder? What is our

lunchtime process? What do we usually eat? Can you help me
describe it?

In the Music Room Amelia told us to ask: "Can you build some instruments?"
Invent instruments with the children. Draw different instruments' sounds. Add
photos of children dancing. More presence of each room's activity would characterize the space, make the children visible, and layer the environment.

In the Lab, Amelia thought we should enrich the collection on the light table
with leaves, polished rocks, shells; more varied papers; transparent and translucent objects. To characterize this room she suggested photographing the children
discovering new materials or using the computer, or while they were in the kaleidoscope (see Figure 5.4). Photographs would layer the environment and explain
the room's function.

The Environment as a Project

Amelia urged us to do a project, Our Environment. It could take 3 months.
We could introduce the idea during full-group-meeting as we summarized with
the children what they had done:

Who went to what area? Say, "Yesterday you did something
fantastic! What do you want to do there tomorrow?" Urge them to

FIGURE 5.4. Walls beginning to change. (Lab)

share their recollections. Add what they remember to the
documentation. Lure them into the project.

Subjects for a project on environment are everywhere. Perusing the Big
Room, she named some: flowers, plants, windows. Then she spied the fish tank:
"Fish! Do fish have names? What is their environment? Draw it. Build it. Play with
it in clay, shadows, wire thread, cardboard, chicken wire, wood." The studio
teacher's presence would stretch our thinking about different materials' potential.

When asked, "What if a child is not interested?" Amelia responded immediately: "If children are not interested, the teacher is at fault. If children do not understand something, the teacher is guilty, not the children. It is *never* the children. The
children are the best. We are ignorant, not them." She sounded like Tiziana. Both
believe that examining the way a teacher offers can reveal the reason for a child's
response.

Our heads were reeling from the analysis of every detail, Amelia's speed in
absorbing and responding to the environment, and the horde of new directions we
could take everywhere. We returned to the Studio. Amelia's flow of suggestions
and our questions continued right through lunch.

HOW TO INVOLVE FAMILIES

Amelia asked if we knew what our parents' jobs were. The teachers explained
that most were on welfare. "Did we," Amelia pushed, "want to hide or offer information about families' realities?" She suggested making an inventory of parents'
jobs, what they do at home. "Make their reality a presence at school." Sensing our
hesitancy to knock on the door of poverty, she talked at length about families.

Communication

Written communication between school and families means messages going
from school and coming from home. If families do not have the necessary supplies,
teachers should send gift bags with paper, pencils, and glue, inviting parents to
prepare a message to the school. Then, at school prepare messages in response.
Begin, "Dear parents, . . ." Children should sign them, draw on them. There should
be a big traffic—messages flying to home and from home constantly—everything
done with the children.

Post current communication alongside the school's calendar and map. Store
past communication in a box labeled To Families. Put a panel, Messages for Home,
in the Greeting Room to post the communication. Engage the children in helping
write the messages: "We are collecting ideas to build instruments. Do you have
ideas?" Write them down, have children illustrate them, and send them home!
Another message might be, "We need stones for . . . ." Xerox it! It goes home! Or,
"We are talking about Washington. Can you help us collect postcards, maps, city
notices?" Or, "We are collecting different color things. Can you help us? We need
your support." She surmised 15 or 20 families might respond. "Try!" Amelia demanded. Don't say, "They can't." Find a way. Use whatever they send.

Another way to involve parents in activities is is by asking them to do research. Amelia emphasized: Request something from everyone, even if only five respond. Accept everything with pride. A little thing is a big achievement. Accept it step-by-step. If it doesn't work, assume it is the teacher's fault. Don't say, "Parents don't do it because they are not interested." Keep trying. Don't stop the process! Be positive. Anything is a big achievement. "It's better to begin on a Friday because weekends give families more time. Send the same message to every family." She was coaching us in the art of relationship building.

Amelia reminded us of an important way to communicate: calling home when a child is sick. It comforts families to know the school is thinking about their child even when he is absent. Amelia suggested calling home with the sick child's best friend.

Objects

Invite parents to send some small object from home. Put it on a shelf with a label: "This is from (child's) home." Whatever the child brings is okay—tea bag, coke bottle, bag of chips, receipt from shopping—it's enough; it is something from home. Add children's words, why they decided to bring this object. Reminding us about letters, Amelia insisted, "Anyone can collect letters from newspapers or magazines. Start with a small provocation, but start, and do it frequently." Ask if parents can cut stamps from envelopes for the Communication Center. Immediately prepare a letter to parents using their stamps, showing that you value material from home.

Ask families for lots of help collecting materials for school. Then, send something home—glue a shell to a tube, wrap it in fancy paper, label it: For mommy, mommy and daddy, or grandma.

Songs

Amelia asked if parents knew the songs the children frequently sang, and offered this suggestion:

> Write a book, illustrated by children, with their favorite songs to give families on a special occasion. Ask, "Do you want to put your name on the front or back? on the drawing? or on another piece of paper entirely?" Let the child decide.

Amelia advised writing children's comments on acetate, using a delicate marker to make the book beautiful.

Reports

In Reggio, rather than reporting on children's progress by measuring ability, teachers describe personality and, especially, how children change. Photos, words, work samples, which Amelia repeatedly urged us to collect, become the basis for telling families about their children.

AND MORE TO COME

Our heads overflowed! Amelia had provided specific advice using every-thing in the environment as departure points. Her focus on the nuances of particu-lar activities suggested dozens of ways in which to expand them. Her explanations of different materials' aesthetic possibilities opened our eyes to the importance of materials. The variety of options she had presented gave us a handle on how to elicit children's individual strengths and reflect their different personalities. Amelia had also considered everything—space, procedures, activities—from the families' perspective. Were we not so stimulated, we might have felt exhausted. But it was our school, our work, our children Amelia had analyzed. The immediacy of her comments and their pertinence to us were highly motivating.

The time seemed on the one hand to stop—we were covering so much so quickly—and on the other to fly—there was so much more we still wanted to know. The session elicited a host of specific questions. Those questions and Amelia's an-swers are the subject of the next chapter.

CHAPTER 6

A Harvest of Answers

We [educators] are not getting the retention, understanding, and active use of knowledge that we want [from students]. . . . what do we do instead? The research and experience of educators, psychologists, and sociologists . . . offer a clear answer, the harvest of what might be called an emerging new science of teaching and learning.

David Perkins

Many of the slides I had shown the prior spring and others Amelia had presented on Friday night contained images that we could not decipher. We barely had the words to question them, much less a sense of the contexts that had elicited them or the processes of which they were part. Some of the slides portrayed complex murals, while others showed intriguing shadow play. Some depicted documentation. Others showed processes—groups of children working together or with their teachers. We needed to know the story behind each of these slides. So, having focused for several hours on Amelia's responses to the MELC and her expansive suggestions, it was now our turn to ask questions.

Finally, there was only one question left: What to do first? The answer to that question was evident in what we did immediately after Amelia's visit. But, predictably, once we began to use her suggestions, more questions emerged. Fortunately, Amelia returned for a second session later in the spring. She was as intrigued to see what her advice had stimulated as we were eager for more information. Our questions, Amelia's answers and our change in focus after her visit, and how we continued the dialogue are the subjects of this chapter.

OUR TURN TO ASK

Amelia addressed our specific questions. We had so many it was hard to know where to begin. We had questions about procedures and techniques. There were images that had puzzled us since we studied my slides a year earlier. And the images Amelia showed the night before as well as her critique and specific suggestions raised new questions.

Murals

How are the huge murals made? Amelia explained that murals begin as an exploration of materials. There is a process. First, start with paper the size of half a table. Have one child on each of three sides, three children working in three different spaces. Comment on what you are doing. Offer a provocation: "Why don't you help her? Yvonne needs help. Could *you* help?" Each time, start with different groups, different friends, different materials, different provocations. Repeat this 10, 20, 30 times.

Later create a larger mural by putting table-sized paper on the floor. Decide which tools and materials children will use to leave traces: different size brushes? stamps? rollers? drawing materials? collage? Start informally, making marks, not something that can be recognized. Initially it's just the pleasure of playing with materials.

Transitions

We asked how to make the transition from morning full-group meeting to work. Amelia called this a "situation in movement," explaining that children are ready for a good transition. In dismissing the meeting tell the children what you have in mind for the morning. Organize everything with the children by involving them in the plan.

For example, if you are doing a project to characterize the environment, tell that to the children. Two different small groups can discuss the environment in two different spaces, five going with Sonya, five with Wendy. Ask, "Who would like to come with me?" Then say, "Now we are going to go around the school, discover all our activities, and describe them."

Tour the school with the groups; show the children the location of things; have them show you things. Don't say, "This is . . . That is . . ." Ask questions to elicit their ideas: "Do you remember what we did?" If your tour includes looking at a project, be sure the children who took part are in the group so they can tell you! Decisions about how to describe the environment are neither the children's nor the teachers'. Each has a different perspective; both are important. Decisions made together are more likely to sustain children's involvement.

Amelia emphasized that a transition is a good time to visit a project in progress, to look at documentation, to review an experience.

Forming Small Groups

The transition from full-group meeting to small-group projects prompted the obvious question: How do you form groups? Wendy asked if selecting children for projects showed favoritism or discrimination, by including some but not others. Amelia assured us, "Composing groups is not discriminating. Other children will do other things. The issue of favoritism is an adult problem." She stressed the importance of each child's emerging through different activity, that each must have something specially his in the school, but something different. Differences are strength.

Forming small groups, we learned, is one of the many keys to the Reggio Approach. Always a matter for intense consideration, Reggio teachers spend considerable time discussing the selection of children, since different teachers' perspectives are essential for good choices. Which child's interest was revealed in something he said? Which child's from something she brought from home? Did this child possess a skill necessary to realize a particular end? Were there strong bonds among group members? Such bonds were fostered. Could a child hesitant to use a particular material be encouraged by others' enthusiasm? The need to form groups carefully provided impetus for teachers' thoughtful observation and note-taking. The process was reciprocal: observe each individual's activities, preferences, friendships, skills; then use your observations to reinforce the child's tendencies.

Orienting New Families

Concerned about our lack of family involvement, we asked how Reggio schools involve families. Amelia described how, when a family decides to enroll, they meet with their child's two teachers in the spring of the prior year. Someone else, with prepared activities, stays with the child to provoke his interests and observe his responses. In this way, the child discovers the school by being with the teachers and using some of the materials, during three or four different visits, before he starts next fall. The teachers have the opportunity to begin to know the child. Simultaneously, other teachers elicit information from the parents to form a portrait of the child's habits, attitudes, and desires. The two sets of teachers compare notes—of the child's and parents' responses. Then the teachers tell children what in the school is of particular interest. Based on the families' information, teachers buy new toys so each child can have a connection to home and find something familiar.

Summer Books. The teachers use books they make themselves, called Summer Books, to fan entering 3-year-olds' desire for new experiences, to alleviate their fear of leaving their parents, and to help prepare the family. The books, like so much else, connect to a web of activities, all part of the introduction-to-school process. During their spring meeting, teachers present each family with the Summer Book, encouraging them to fill the books, describing places for notes and questions—about birthdays, family friends, experiences they will have over the summer. Teachers take extreme care to make the books beautiful, a treasure of images and words, specially designed for each child.

The empty book is full of questions to elicit the parents' story of their child. Pages are designed so the family can add photographs of themselves, their pets, their summer holiday, their activities in the town center. On other pages the family can make notes, paste postcards, and other memorabilia. These become links between school and home as each child arrives in September with his own history, enriching the teachers' understanding of his life. In fall, a school party immediately draws children and parents into the new experience.

Bags of History. Amelia described the big plastic bag of children's productions, another link in a child's chain of experience. These Summer Bags, also a present from school to family, expand teachers' contact with families and arouse families' new interests in the school. Transparent bags are sent home at year-end; in September they are returned full of memories, stuff parents put together to answer teachers' questions. Teachers study the contents to discover a child's strongest interests. For example, if children bring lots of material about summer, teachers might do projects on seasons. Bags continue to be used, and by year-end contain a family's and child's memories.

Bags going to and fro, full of children's ideas and feelings, link school and home. A bag might return with a mother's bracelet or a sibling's drawing. Other messages, whatever interests a child—change of seasons, family stories, cats—go home in the bag, a piece of her history. Because bags are transparent, others can see the histories, but not touch unless the owner concurs.

Bags and books spark dialogues. For example, teachers provoke conversations among a small group of children on a subject gleaned from a bag or a book. As children take over the conversation, the teacher moves on to start a conversation among another group. We conceded these activities would mean more after the MELC families became more involved. "But," Amelia queried, "do you know whether your families have photos at home? Have you planned an activity with families' photos? Put them up [see Figure 6.1]. Or animals? Ask! Get their photos!" Everything Amelia urged us to add throughout the environment would both inform parents about activities at school and arouse their interest, stimulating them to become involved.

Whether we used these techniques immediately, Reggio teachers' rich repertoire gave us ideas, and were springboards for much that we would do. It was eye-opening to hear so many ways to build connections between a school and its families.

It was now after 4 P.M. Saturday afternoon. If Amelia were exhausted, it didn't show. The teachers still had questions.

FIGURE 6.1. Parents engrossed seeing photos of themselves on panels. (Hallway to Nap Room)

Light and Shadow

Many slides had spurred our curiosity about light and shadows. We asked how to do projects in this exciting medium. Amelia launched into detailed instructions:

Make a box and install a 5-watt light. Opposite the light make holes with different-sized nails, including pinholes. Project children's drawings in front of this box; it will appear that a snowstorm of light has fallen on them. Engage children in drawing and playing with light. Project it on the floor and ceiling, on the children, on their drawings.

She described how to use slides with transparent gels:

Light alone will cast a black shadow. Add colored slides with a single projector, then with two projectors. Project color on children's bodies. Project images on their bodies. Project beautiful slides—flowers, animals, the desert, outer space, underwater—and provocative slides—a fountain or lion. Project slides all around the room. Play! Ask, "How does this work? What is going on? Where does this come from?"

Go outside and observe shadows. Make shadows with objects. Hold one object at different angles. Cast shadows from the front and back. Have children guess the object.

Inside make a construction of objects. Depending on an object's relation to the screen, it can be tiny or huge. A child can become bigger than an adult. Make an image of a cat, its tail, whiskers, movements. At first, its movement alone will interest the children. Project a moving fish-on-a-stick using a light blue gel as a mask. First, teachers must play with shadows, not to teach what they learn, but to familiarize themselves with shadows' properties and potential and to become adept at using slide and opaque projectors. Shadow play will be exuberant, full of laughter.

Amelia was giving us a wealth of ways to involve children both in playful experiences and in the science and art of light, shadow, color, illusion, and imagination.

SHADOW PLAY IN REGGIO

Amelia's advice about shadow play was based on a rich history, as the following story shows. I had the opportunity to observe shadow play in Reggio in June 1994 when I visited the toddlers' class at Il Girotonda, an infant center for 69 three-month- to three-year-olds. When I arrived, the toddlers were just waking from their nap. The teacher had lowered the shadow screen and children were gathering in front. She began: "*Alors! Attenzione!* (Now then! Pay attention!)" That afternoon I watched an entire class, 21 toddlers, 15–24 months, entranced for over an hour and a half.

Toddlers and Shadows

From behind the screen the teacher began to project slides, the room dark except for the projector. As children awoke, they joined the group until all were watching the screen. Images appeared—beautifully colored fish, graceful sea anemone, exotic coral, other forms of sea life. Each remained longer than I thought children would attend. Although I feared they might become impatient—the slides were numerous and they were so young—the children were intent, not restless.

"Ooohs" and "aahs" erupted whenever a new image appeared. I thought the noise might distract, but was wrong again. The children were keenly attentive to the slowly changing images repeating over and over. No one stirred, except to exclaim appreciatively at the images. Thirty to forty minutes passed.

The teacher brought three or four children to her side of the screen, encouraging them to move with the images. I feared the entire group might rush to join the few, or the teacher would lose control. Wrong again.

The teacher encouraged more and more children to come behind the screen until half the group was participating while the other half was watching, observing their friends' silhouettes among the sea life. Then the teacher introduced a box of props—cutouts of fish, starfish, sea plants, each with a handle. She encouraged the children to engage their props with the images and each others' props. Finally only three or four children, who preferred to be spectators, not actors, were left. Now the spectators viewed a dance of children and sea creatures. Another half hour passed.

The teacher then changed the tenor, introducing new slides—an empty grey ocean, a gigantic shark with a gaping mouth. And she introduced a new prop, a headdress of a shark's head which one child wore. She encouraged the "shark" to chase the "small fish." The toddlers shrieked as shark-child chased fish-children. As before, I grew uneasy; however, nothing untoward outside the context of the play happened.

Gradually, the teacher collected the props. I was full of questions, but held back, thinking the transition needed her full attention. She rolled up the screen and turned on the lights as, on their own, the toddlers became involved in other activities.

Tentatively, I asked if I could return later to ask questions. "No! Why not now? Ask me now!" she exclaimed. I began: "What stimulated the choice of images? How did children so young learn to attend for so long? What accounted for their absorption? their orderly behavior?" In English, the teacher explained that in the fall a child had brought a book from home about sea life. A tremendous, unexpected hit, the children asked for it daily. The parent let the book remain at school all year. The teacher had not even planned to introduce the sea!

Significance of Shadows

Shadow screens, a favorite activity in all Reggio schools, are used often, in many ways, frequently with props. Children especially enjoy images reflecting a beloved book. The toddlers I happened to see had become so involved, they were preparing a year-end show for their parents. I had seen a kind of dress rehearsal.

Mariano Dolci, Reggio schools' expert puppet master, recounts myths, legends, customs, and taboos associated with shadows in cultures worldwide. Significantly, many languages use the same word for soul and shadow. Interest in the shadow-soul did not wane with the declining belief in magic. It just manifested differently in various literary and cinematographic motifs: death, life, geometry, shadow plays, time. Infinite references to shadows throughout man's history illustrate that shadow, hovering between the physical and metaphysical, greatly stimulated imagination, reason, and logic. Reggio children precociously notice shadows, interacting with them frequently. What enthralls children? The greater the number and variety of games, the more ways adults use shadows, the more children notice (Spaggiari et al., 1990).

The following comments from Reggio infant centers and preschools reflect children's experience with shadows:

> "When it rains, there is no shadow. It goes inside us because it doesn't want to get wet." (Children, 2-10–3-6).
> "A shadow is like a night that comes when the sun is out."
> "It's the same as when you look at yourself in the mirror, except that there's nothing inside, it's all black and doesn't laugh."
> "Your shadow is like a projected movie that follows you."
> "Even small rocks make a shadow; bigger ones do it better." (Children, 3-10–5-3).
> "It's flying! When I jump it flies." (Children, 3-8–4-3).
> "Everything makes a shadow, even a space ship; when it passes over and under planets and there's a star that illuminates it, it is reflected on the planets." (Child, 5-6). (Spaggiari et al., 1990, pp. 31–89)

In the poetry and science of the children's comments is evidence of their teachers' study and respect for humans' long tradition of interactions with shadows, their intentional use of shadows to pique children's thinking. The toddlers' play I had observed hadn't just happened, but resulted from their teachers' philosophical interests and teaching practices: using shadows to provoke, then carefully observing children's responses. Give-and-take—child to provocation, teacher to child—determines what happens. It is spontaneous choreography. Indeed, it is a new art form.

Reggio's commitment to time as a resource supports the shadow work. Teachers allow activities to flow, following children's interest, extending their concentration. Mihaly Csikszentmihalyi (1993), father of flow theory, says:

> "Flow" usually happens . . . when we are actively involved in a difficult enterprise, in a task that stretches our physical or mental abilities. Any activity can do it. Working on a challenging job, riding the crest of a tremendous wave, and teaching one's child the letters of the alphabet are the kinds of experiences that focus our whole being in a harmonious rush of energy. . . . When challenges are high and personal skills are used to the utmost, we experience this rare state of consciousness. (pp. xxxi–iv)

People are "in flow" when an activity is neither too challenging nor too simple, when it keeps them on edge, not so hard that it frustrates, but not so simple that it bores. People in flow lose track of time and even forget to eat (Csikszentmihalyi, 1990). Current learning theory recognizes flow as highly conducive to learning. Reggio teachers and children are frequently in flow.

WHAT SHOULD WE DO MONDAY?

The afternoon was fast waning. There had been an outpouring of information. The teachers asked one final question, "What should we do *now*?" Amelia was thoughtful:

> If I were you now . . . Think about the symposium. Talk with the children about it. Ask, "Would you like to show all these visitors—from Washington, the United States, other countries—about your school?"
>
> Start with the environment. Tour the school as teachers. Look at the floor plan. Then meet, inventory your ideas, categorize them. Decide what you are going to attack. Figure out how you will involve children in the process. Start with the goal of changing the rooms' labels by adding titles in children's words and writing. You, the teachers, have to organize everything first.
>
> Then involve children: "Now we want new descriptions of our environment. Can you help us?" Collect their words. Reread your notes to connect their words to your inventory. Likewise, connect your ideas to what the children are saying, to their parents' ideas, to activities in the classroom and at home. Tell the children and write to the parents: "We want to start from . . . We want to improve this . . . How will we do it? Who will do it? What process will we use?"

Amelia emphasized that step-by-step organization about everyone who will be involved is really important—organization, not improvisation. Change is not easy. It demands a huge effort as well as ideas, desire, need, and above all strength. Nothing is easy. But teachers' pleasure is in direct proportion to their effort.

"Where would I start?" Amelia pondered. In the Greeting Room with names of children, of teachers, calendars, the class schedule, more information for parents, more space for parents. Make the space precious, move the African newspaper from the Greeting Room to the Parent Room. It has meaning culturally, but here you need space to display the *school's* culture. Make everything open—the children, the staff, the schedule: Lunch is at — o'clock; nap is at —. We arrive at —. We end at—. You are not making a daily schedule, you are drawing families and visitors into the life here.

Finally Amelia said, "Enough! Stop!" It was long after 5.

The Changes Begin

Reflecting on Amelia's first visit to the MELC, we agreed she had provided a rich feast. Her critique and her outpouring—what happens in Reggio schools, what we could do in ours—let us sail through the spring. She had stressed that everything has a process, a context, a connection to other things. She had urged us to involve children in all the processes, to work with them to put everything in context, to explore connections, to make links visible. She had answered our questions, specified techniques for many activities, provided precise words to use. By the end of her visit, the teachers were eager to put the ideas into practice.

First Step: the Environment

Two days after Amelia left, the teachers began. First, they decided to keep a daily log, titled "What Happened On . . ." showing all children's activities. Teachers would add information from their work with small groups, thus building a comprehensive record of what all children did every day.

The teachers pounced on Amelia's suggestion to layer the environment, describing it in children's words and drawings, adding children's photos, collages, and constructions, vastly increasing materials everywhere—pens, pencils, symbols, games, blocks, and eventually a huge quantity of items from children's homes, many stored in jars also from their homes. They also began to take small groups of children on tours to revisit the panels.

Monday, March 8. The teachers sent a letter home asking for glass jars. Four children helped write it (see Figure 6.2). For weeks, jars poured in. The children soaked off the labels and discussed where to use the jars as vases in the Dining Room; as containers for materials in the Studio; for numbers and letters in the Big Room; for symbols, numbers, letters, and stamps in the Communication Center.

Tuesday, March 9. The teachers followed Amelia's urging to do a project on the school environment. They began tours of the school, eliciting what children knew, taking notes on children's comments, using comments for descriptions written by everyone during full-group meetings. Five children described the Music Room.

Wendy: What happens in this room?
Tiara (4-7): We come in and play drums. People can dance here also. They can play all kinds of music . . . and they play the guitar.
Quatesha (4-7): Sometimes we come in with groups. Miss Wendy come in here all the time.
Jameana (5-5): We have drums, guitar, and shakers . . . There are all kinds of music instruments in here . . . They get real hot from dancing.
Alex (4-9): I like the map of Africa.
Donnell (5-5): I like the way they hit the drums.

FIGURE 6.2. In response, jars poured in for weeks.

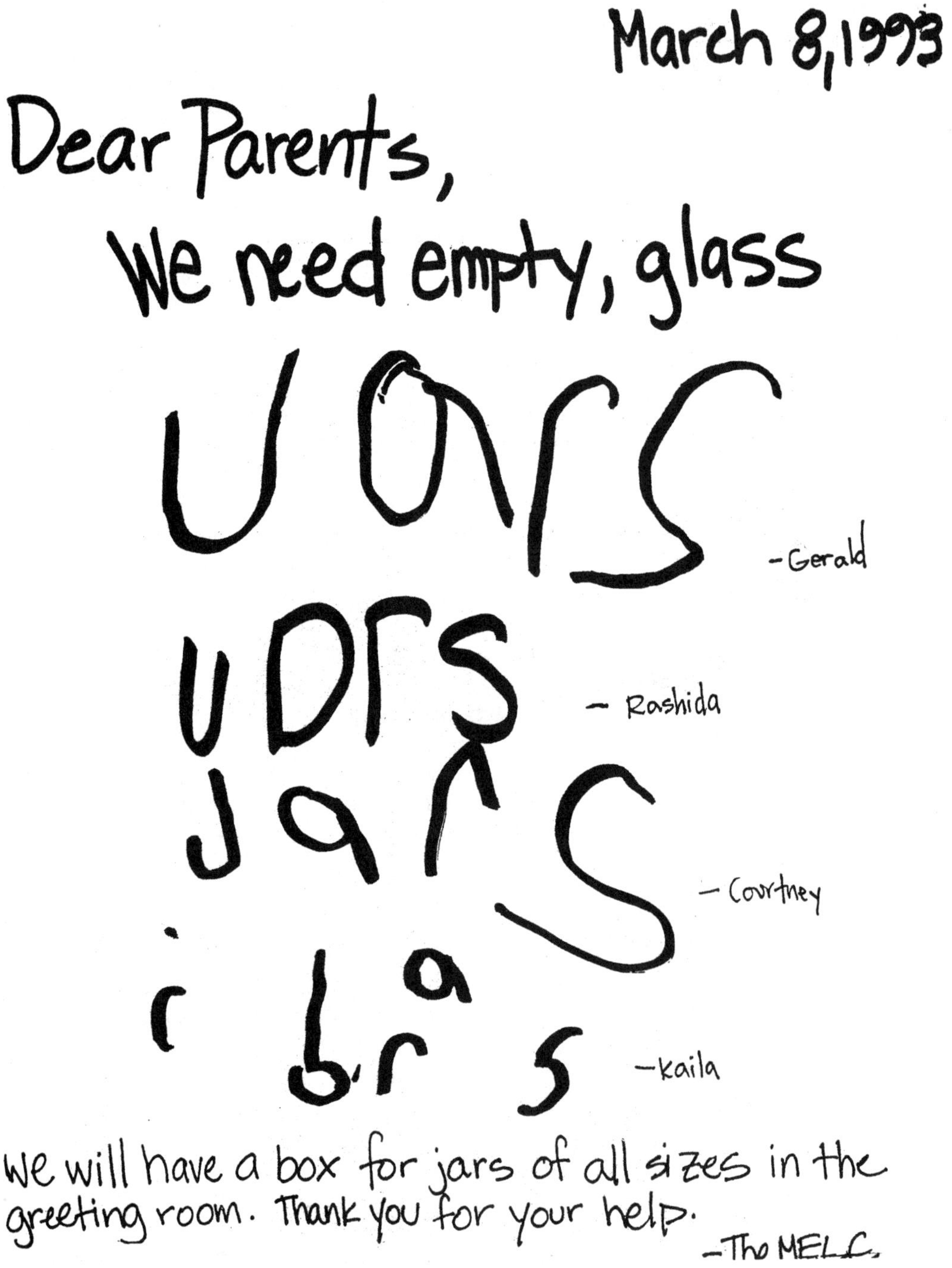

March 8, 1993

Dear Parents,
    We need empty, glass

U ars

—Gerald

U Drs

— Rashida

Jars

— Courtney

i b r a s

—Kaila

We will have a box for jars of all sizes in the
greeting room. Thank you for your help.
                                    —The MELC.

Friday, March 19. Teachers replaced the text outside each room with panels of children's words and drawings, and reworked the Greeting Room. Among the many changes, they hung photos of each of the staff with children's descriptions and drawings. With the children they wrote a letter asking for family photographs. Letter writing spilled into the Housekeeping area. Six children worked in the Studio papier mâchéing jars that they later painted for the Dining Room.

Tuesday, March 23. Six children worked on describing and drawing Genet. The children would vote on which drawing best represented each teacher. Drawings would hang in the Greeting Room for more layering.

Wednesday, March 24. Brandi (4-1) and Tyresha (3-0) described photos of their families to Jennifer, then drew family members, beginning a project reflected on a large panel, our families and us.

The Environment Project began to make the school look layered. Now you entered to face the large photo-portraits with a medley of miniature collages, one beside each child's name. Instead of typeset text, crisp white panels hung outside each room with children's descriptions, their drawings of goings-on, and photos of them working there.

MOMENTUM GROWS

We had asked Amelia to return and 7 weeks later she did. The teachers requested that she focus on materials. Again, she showed slides, described techniques, emphasized that children's first experiences with materials should not produce a specific thing, that children must know materials before they can use them purposefully toward specific ends. Amelia left us with this thought: "A teacher who says, 'I am a good teacher,' is in trouble. A good teacher is frequently troubled, in doubt, frustrated. Perfection does not exist. Everyone needs help."

New Projects

Amelia's second visit inspired the teachers to start a variety of new projects. The results of some would remain exhibited for over a year; others would evolve into new projects that would continue the next year. All increased the teachers' confidence in using Reggio practices.

The Lemon Tree. In the Studio, Jennifer, Tyresha (3-0), and Maulana (3-7) suspended life-size papier mâché lemons from a huge branch. Called The Lemon Tree, it hung all next year, its bright forms a focal point.

Pets. Renée (4-10), LaShay (5-6), and Donnnell (5-5) continued projects about Coco, accompanying Wendy to the vet while Coco was neutered, writing, drawing, and reporting on the experience. Children also became involved in the fishes' life.

The Ambulance. On April 29, Jennifer, Shameka (6-0), Alonzo (5-3), and Jameana (5-6) continued a project stimulated by the TV show *9-1-1*. It began with

Wendy's asking what the children wanted to know. The ambulance emerged as their main interest. The small group boarded a real ambulance, made a sizable one in the Studio, and chose to stage a puppet show rather than a play about the trip.

The Capitol. A newspaper clipping sent by a parent stimulated a few children to begin a complex project with Sonya on the Capitol. The project spanned many months, eventually involving almost all 36 children, working in small groups on various aspects. Its documentation covered all the walls in the long hallway to the Dining Room, spilling onto adjoining walls as the project continued the following year.

Shadow Play. Amelia had urged us to use a shadow screen, and on May 17 the teachers began. First, they experimented with the equipment themselves, putting colored pieces of theater gel, lace, netting, and other translucent or semiopaque objects on the bed of an opaque projector and projecting the colors and designs on their own bodies. They determined which materials had the best effect and the relative positions for light source and people. Jennifer recalled some years later, "It was not straightforward!" Subsequently, three children staged a shadow show for a large audience of parents. The teachers noted that the work needed improvement, but at least they had begun.

Reaching Beyond Our Walls

The Reggio Emilia Symposium, hosted by TNLC, was at hand. From June 9–12, 1993, 403 educators from 33 states and 4 foreign countries attended 3 days of lectures by Loris Malaguzzi, Sergio Spaggiari, Carlina Rinaldi, Tiziana Filippini, and Amelia Gambetti, as well as dialogues between them and leading American early childhood educators. Most who attended also visited the MELC. One visitor requested, "Please continue to spread the message of Reggio Emilia. It empowers children and increases teacher understanding." Another exclaimed, "My very favorite experience was seeing the Model Early Learning Center at the Children's Museum." Another commented, "I learned that getting the collaborative process off the ground is *hard*—I need patience." Their responses affirmed our effort.

Our reputation was growing. On August 9, 1993, an article appeared in the *Christian Science Monitor* by Lee Adair Lawrence, a freelance writer who lived nearby and knew about the MELC. Entitled "An Italian Import for Early Education," it included a photo, descriptions of some projects, and reference to the MELC's uniqueness in serving economically disadvantaged children.

The symposium left the staff buoyant and ready to charge ahead. Lawrence's article raised their spirits even higher. But most exciting of all was the agreement we had made with Amelia: She would spend the following year in residence at the MELC.

CHAPTER 7

Apprenticeship with Amelia

Outcomes are latent in the dynamic structure of the system we have or may adopt: they will inexorably emerge.

Stafford Beer

Amelia tutored the MELC teachers in Reggio practices for 23 weeks during school year 1993–94. She worked as master-consulting-teacher-in-residence with them daily—observing, critiquing, urging, praising, modeling, helping them understand the philosophy minute by minute. She found them "completely open and available." In this pivotal year, the most striking change was the teachers' growth under her tutelage.

In the beginning the close scrutiny made us feel unprotected, naked. In Amelia's third week she asked everyone to make lists, daily, of children's activities and notes on what they said, then use these as the basis for a planning process. We struggled to understand how. In this chapter I explain what we did, show how the teachers learned to help children make choices, and describe how, by year-end, we had changed.

VULNERABILITIES

The first weeks in September 1993 were rough for everyone. Amelia was prepared by long experience, but the teachers were new at it all. They felt vulnerable, she unsure.

Jennifer had a very difficult time. While Sonya had cried over the school's early chaos or pain in a child's life, Jennifer now cried as the adaptation caused deep uncertainty about her role. Sonya and Jennifer were the same age, both single, highly educated, attractive, intelligent, and equally desirous for success. They would have to learn to collaborate without feeling threatened.

Wendy faced the challenge of meeting her family's needs as well as the MELC's, which multiplied with the Reggio adaptation. She was calm and wise. If she felt Sonya's anguish or Jennifer's insecurity, it was not obvious. If she felt isolated as an African American teacher older than her colleagues, one would never know it.

Genet and Deborah, beautiful young African American women, had begun as aides, both showing promise. Could Genet admit what she did not know? Could Deborah admit her discomfort? Could Wendy and Jennifer admit they were less skillful writers than Sonya? Could Sonya and Wendy admit they needed Jennifer's expertise to use materials? Could Jennifer and Sonya admit Wendy was more experienced working with young children? Could they trust each other enough to express fears, face confrontation, react to a colleague's honest comment without being defensive?

I was concerned with administrative matters throughout the TNLC. I relinquished the program's guidance to Amelia, and became an observer, the teachers' cheerleader, the school's ombudsman. I continued to negotiate its financial support and assure that its other needs were met. Amelia and I met regularly once a week, more if needed, to discuss issues she brought to me—some involved teachers, others parents. Together we made sure that we communicated fully with Loris Malaguzzi and others in Reggio. I worked with Maurice Sykes, our D.C. Public Schools (DCPS) liaison, to forge teacher education programs for his staff and to assure that the MELC played a substantive role in helping him achieve his goals for improving early childhood programs in the public schools. I worked closely with Amelia and the teachers developing MELC Days, a new program for other educators to learn about the MELC. I especially wanted to ensure that MELC Days not pressure the teachers or impact the children negatively.

I stopped writing memos to the staff and waited. There was no one moment when, all of a sudden, we "got it." Changes happened gradually.

SCRUTINIZING THE MELC

Amelia put every aspect of the school under scrutiny—activities, family involvement, using time, everything. Big issues surfaced daily.

The First Ten Days

Amelia said, "I asked to observe for a week to 10 days. Like a shadow, I followed everyone everywhere and took many notes. The director . . . gave me complete freedom, . . . a big message of trust" (Lewin, 1998, p. 345). The teachers asked Amelia why she was observing; it would be more useful if she simply answered their questions. Amelia explained she was not there to evaluate, but to learn about the MELC. She asked the teachers to list their questions, what they wanted to know about her experiences, their expectations for her residency.

Ten days later they had their first meeting. They discussed Amelia's observations and the teachers' questions. Immediately they realized that if they were to meet their goal of forging themselves into a team, everyone must know what everyone else was doing. So Amelia asked them to make the lists and take the daily notes. It was a huge responsibility. Had they balked, it would have created an impasse, but everyone agreed.

The following week Amelia asked the teachers to compare their notes, discuss the differences, and reach consensus about what the notes suggested for tomorrow's activities. This was threatening. The process of comparing required each teacher to express her own opinions, and they might have entirely different opinions about the same occurrence and might disagree about what to do next. Amelia understood that unless the teachers dealt with such conflicts, expressed their confusions, acknowledged their mistakes, they could not talk honestly about what they were doing or why. She understood that they needed to learn not just from their own experiences but through one another's, that they had to negotiate their differences, that doing so would forge them into a team. She knew it would be difficult: "It is easier to say *Yes*, and then do what you want . . . than to say *No*, explain [your] motivation . . . and together reach agreement" (Lewin, 1998, pp. 345–346).

People in the workplace rarely express honest opinions. The MELC was no exception. To the teachers, Amelia's insistence on honesty was especially threatening; they feared that honest remarks about one another would sound insensitive. They did not yet trust one another, so honesty felt risky: It could generate criticism of *you*.

Phasing-in

Phasing-in means gradually adding children until all are in attendance. The process had been key to a smooth start in prior years. This year, from day one, there was an air of expectation: waiting for Amelia; anticipating the return of children being phased in; planning parties and making surprises for them. Cemetria (4-7) and Terrell (4-3) drew an enormous fish from which a group constructed a huge pinata as the centerpiece for a party. Excitement mounted as it took shape (see Figure 7.1).

Phasing-in reduced the risk of children's misbehaving by providing time for teachers to review procedures with small groups. Visitors on MELC Days

FIGURE 7.1. The first children phased in created a huge surprise for new children. (Dining Room)

questioned whether there was hitting or fighting, behaviors some either expected from young children or had experienced in their own schools. The teachers answered no, attributing it to the fact that the phase-in period gave them time to review the rules with small groups. Because of parents' needs for child care, not all schools allow phasing-in and we always felt a little guilty that we had this luxury. But, from the school's opening through the beginning of the current school year, we clung to it tenaciously to be sure we settled the children. The question always arose of how quickly to phase in. In 1993–94 it took 8 weeks for all 36 children, reflecting the teachers' reluctance to handle all of them at once, understandable given earlier years' behavior problems. The following year everyone was phased in in only 3 weeks, reflecting the teachers' new assurance.

How Activities Changed

Preparing to welcome students who would be phased in took lots of time in fall 1993, according to the teachers' weekly activity summaries. Numerical analysis cannot quantify the thousands of exchanges that occur daily in a classroom, but it can offer a different perspective. Counting only what the teachers recorded in their summaries, 28% of activities in the first eight weeks related to phasing-in and an equal percentage to language. The balance was spread over scores of different activities.

The accumulation of daily summaries revealed interesting patterns. For example, the focus of activities shifted after Amelia's arrival; activities that had rarely happened increased dramatically, from one project and one instance of family involvement in the first three weeks of school to seven projects and 13 instances of family involvement in the 5 weeks immediately after she arrived. Amelia found 21 occasions between October 1 and 26 for messages to be sent home, sometimes two daily—letters, forms, lists, memos, invitations, minutes of meetings. Messages prepared families to become involved before they ever set foot in the school, awakening their interest in what their children were doing.

Reporting Back. Reporting back is the "story of what we did," a new activity Amelia introduced during end-of-morning group meeting. Reporting back enabled the full class to hear what small groups had done that morning, stimulating children's interest in one another's projects. Equally important, it provided practice in speaking and listening, essential prerequisites for learning to read. Reporting back became a daily activity.

Seeding Projects. Many activities early in the year seeded later projects. Collecting information from museum exhibits became a project to learn about the museum. Teachers' observation of children's interest in what was happening outside seeded the Fall project. When the children spontaneously brought leaves, teachers played a game they called What To Do. The game sparked the idea to send a letter asking families to help collect evidence of fall. Thirty-four families (almost 95%) responded, evidence of fall poured in, and a long project evolved.

Discussions seeded projects; discussions about family photos and children's descriptions of the relationships they portrayed seeded a Families project. The panel about that project drew families into the school because they enjoyed seeing their photos beautifully displayed along with the children's descriptions and drawings of themselves, other relatives, and their homes. Discussion about the fish and aquarium seeded the Fish project. Drawings seeded projects; portraits of the librarian and the teachers became a project to give the Greeting Room more evidence of children's work. Objects from home seeded projects; examination of letters that parents cut from newspapers seeded the Alphotography project.

Using Time

With Amelia's coaching, the prior year's loose schedule tightened. Almost an hour, 8:00 to 8:50, became a time for teachers to meet. Teachers became clearer about their responsibilities and as a result purposeful about what they were doing. Each teacher now had a place and a function in starting the day.

Arrival and Breakfast. Miss Wendy sat in the Big Chair in the Greeting Room and gave hugs (see Figure 7.2). In the Big Room Sonya helped children hang up coats and, as part of the transition from home, watched as they went down the hall to breakfast. Before breakfast Jennifer continued yesterday's activities in the Studio with a few children. At the Book Sharing table Deborah received and arranged books to go home that day. Genet oversaw breakfast in the Dining Room. Use of time became intentional, changes reflecting teachers' growing understanding of their craft, a new precision about *what* they were doing, *when* to do it, and *why*.

Breakfast became a favorite time. The children found it exciting to reconnect with friends. They socialized. Families even came. Teachers really became acquainted with children. Conversations were so long that, as Sonya said, "The cereal got soggy." At first open-ended, over the year breakfast time shortened. By year-end Amelia would say, "Breakfast starts at 9 and at 9:30 is done!"

Meetings. After breakfast and before full-group meeting, as the excitement of socializing calmed, there was a period of adjustment to the classroom. Children might select a book, look at panels, use items from shelves, play with the blocks or trains. As the flow evolved, full-group meeting times changed. What had been none, one, or sometimes two became a regular early meeting, at which teachers might ask questions to retain continuity from day to day, and a regular late meeting to share what had happened that day.

If Jennifer had worked on clay, she brought an example and described what had happened in the Studio. Once, after purchasing games and puzzles with animals because they would be drawing animals in the Studio, Jennifer asked if the children remembered seeing all the animal puzzles, if they wanted to see more, arousing their interest, building their expectations. By mid-October, discussions at full-group meetings changed from talking about random subjects to summarizing what had happened or what might happen in different areas of the school that day or week. Such conversations brought a new focus to activities.

Work Time. Teachers talked frequently with individual children or small groups about details of their current activities, what happened last week, what might happen tomorrow. The choices teachers offered were based on their collective opinions about children's interests, which they discussed during their

FIGURE 7.2. A day begins with Miss Wendy's hug. (Greeting Room)

after-school meetings. Because offers were so thoughtfully considered—from five teachers' perspectives—most children accepted the offers eagerly. Projects and nonproject work occurred simultaneously, projects taking place anywhere, places changing as needs emerged. Children not involved in a project could choose from areas spread over 3,500 square feet in many different rooms. Visitors were always surprised that all areas were available to all children at all times.

If Sonya, Wendy, Jennifer, and Genet were involved in different projects simultaneously, other children worked on their own or in self-formed groups wherever they chose, all overseen by Deborah. Most worked independently. Only three areas required direct supervision—the climbing apparatus, the Music Room, and water play. Within these limits, children could choose freely, even continuing an activity rather than going to the playground, since some teachers remained inside.

When children were on the playground, teachers frequently worked on panels "stealing time," Amelia's phrase for making the most of every minute. Amelia helped us spot wasted time. Four teachers were overseeing lunch: "Do we need four?" Her question raised awareness, freeing one or two to work on something else.

Work time was an hour and a half, maybe longer, depending on a morning's flow. End-of-morning meetings could be brief 10-minute reviews of the day or plans for a trip. A trip could involve the whole class or a group doing a project. If a big discussion began, the meeting could last half an hour and lunch would be later.

Lunch, Afternoon, After School. Lunch began between 11:30 and 12. Children napped from about 1 to 2:30, then had another choice time. From 3:30 to 4 teachers organized the environment with children, storing or replenishing materials, until all the children had gone home. The teachers met after school from 4 to 5, often far later, addressing topics requiring lengthy discussion. Whereas morning meetings dealt with immediate needs—preparation of the day's materials, last looks at hypotheses before plunging in—afternoon meetings covered topics like what might occur in projects, whom to include in small groups, plans for parent meetings or field trips, and who would be away from school. Based on their notes, they surmised who would be where the coming day and determined what supervision children not involved in projects might require. They learned to maintain a high level of awareness among themselves, especially in the morning, making a huge effort to tell each other what they would (probably) be doing.

On October 27, the teachers sent the first Monthly Report to the Director:

> Working with Amelia is amazing, and yes, exhausting! We have been meeting three or four times a week until 6, 7, or 8 at night and then going home to transcribe. There is a notebook with an outline of each meeting. Subjects we address include how to use the dialogues of children, how to support new children, friendships, the organization of our days, meetings; the list goes on and on. We are learning a tremendous amount and feel the experience . . . is invaluable.

Simultaneously they were grappling with how to involve parents, reorganizing the parent-teacher committee, sending home dozens of messages, making a score of panels, and learning to trust one another. It was exhilarating and exhausting.

Gradually, they realized they needed to share their strengths: Jennifer's with materials, Sonya's with words and camera, Wendy's years of experience, Genet's quiet manner, Deborah's ability to keep tabs everywhere. In a word, they realized they needed to *collaborate*. In Amelia's words, they were learning to "slow down." It may seem contradictory to do more by slowing down. It wasn't that they did more, but that everything had a purpose, a new intentionality.

A PLANNING PROCESS EVOLVES

American schools are schedule driven so we find it difficult to grasp how to organize a day without lesson plans and objectives. Americans watch the clock; Reggio educators watch the children. They base planning on what they observe, not on predetermined lessons, and unexpected things happen often. The MELC teachers would learn to plan for the unexpected.

Making Hypotheses

How does one plan for what *might* happen? In after-school meetings the teachers shared their daily notes and what they had transcribed at night. Note by note, carefully considering all their observations, the group hypothesized, or predicted, what might happen next. For example, if they sent a message home requesting evidence of fall, eight children might bring leaves, pods, acorns. If so, teachers would need time to examine everything with the children, to sort the items and discuss characteristics and possible uses of each, to decide what kind of container each required, if they had one, if not, where they might find one. They would need time to fill the containers, to decide where to put them—in the Storeroom? Studio? Big Room?—and time to stow them away. These activities might take days. If children brought nothing, they would have to scratch that hypothesis and use their notes to identify other possible activities.

Observing that the school was "merely going along from day to day," that next activities had little connection to prior activities, Amelia urged the teachers to make more thoughtful observations. This was tough to hear because they were already making such an enormous effort in taking notes, recording, and transcribing. Amelia's observation triggered anguished soul-searching and perplexed discussion: *Why* were the children doing what they did? *Where* should the teachers focus their note taking? *What* should they record? As a result they rethought their entire process. At first they tried making lists, like an inventory, trying to keep track of each child's activities all morning long. But this procedure didn't work; there was too much to track. Instead, they began to make a hypothetical organization for each activity—what *might* occur next week—using the after-school meetings to write all the many ways each listed activity might evolve. This didn't work at all because the volumes of options were overwhelming.

Finally, the teachers decided they needed a system and designed a form to help organize themselves. The form was 8½" × 11" and looked like a calendar of the week, with days in a row across the top and boxes in columns under each day. They discussed what had been done last week and, on each day of the current week, filled in what might happen next, who would do it, and where. A filled-in form showed what a week could be like considering what the children had already done and what they might do next.

A Dynamic Process

During class meetings, teachers used the form to remind themselves and children of what they had been doing or to offer children choices of what to do next. Often, the reminder spurred the children to continue, especially when the teachers said, "Let's go look!" and the children saw what they had done recorded on a panel. (This was possible because simultaneously the teachers were engaged in an enormous effort to make documentation panels.) Whatever children did the teachers noted, discussed, and used as the basis for new hypotheses about tomorrow and the following days, writing everything on the form. What they had written reflected what *had* happened, but what had happened was not what they had predicted. So they crossed it out and inserted what did happen. By week's end, it was illegible to all but the makers. When MELC Day visitors asked to see a form, no one could read it. It was a cacophony of color and movement, like several complex schematics all in one—virtually a solid mass of crossed-out words and different-colored lines running everywhere. It had to be recopied to be legible. Recopied it looked like an ordinary weekly lesson plan. The teachers knew the minute they saw it that it had to change.

The forms were not plans; they contained past activities and possible ones, not planned lessons. They did not say what to do; they were records of what might follow from what had been done and reflected enormous forethought, lengthy discussions, and group consensus: on the one hand . . . ; and if . . . ; but maybe . . . The process allowed for the many eventualities that result from the human tendencies toward unpredictability, novelty, and complexity. At upper grades it would be like throwing away the text and basing next readings on what emerged spontaneously from a class discussion. The process stimulated deep thought about what they were doing and is sometimes called an emergent curriculum.

A System of Forms Becomes a System

Each week's recopied form—what had happened last week—was posted in the Greeting Room. Over time, parents began to rely on these forms to see what had taken place. As use of the form evolved, teachers added names of children having birthdays; "hanging" questions; ongoing projects; activities from outside like the librarian's visit; activities for outside like project-related research. Gradually, they realized they could consider what might happen 1 or 2 weeks hence.

In time, recopied forms chronicled life at school that year, readily available for anyone's review. As the year progressed, it became apparent that several other forms were needed to keep track of the increasingly complex activities. A Month Plan evolved and, to be sure parents were advised, a Monthly Notice of Upcoming Dates; both forms were posted and sent home. Eventually teachers reorganized the Parent Board, establishing a set place to post each form, and added new shelves in the Greeting Room to display folders organized to hold copies of each new form.

Because everyone came to rely on the forms, their use took on structure and the forms became the means to understand how activities impacted each person. For example, children could be involved with two things at once, like exploring a new material with Jennifer and also doing a project with Wendy. This affected hypotheses. If two teachers wanted Quatesha, she would look at them as if they were crazy, as if to say, "How can I be in two places at once?" The system guarded against cross-purposes, and ensured that teachers pursued the most significant activities. In sum, the teachers had learned the difference between lesson planning and process planning, for that is what hypotheses are—a way to plan a process. By year-end a new system was in place.

A COMMITMENT TO CHOICE

Choosing is the essence of being human, a volitional act that reflects a young child's developing self-awareness. Choice is synonymous with free will, and is the basis for judgment and morality. Encouraging children to choose develops their awareness of how their minds work, and helps their teachers perceive their innate differences, revealing what Gardner (1983) calls *intelligences*. In order to choose, a child must know what choices are available; as Reggio educators say, a child must "read" the environment, know what exists in each area of the school, as well as everything's potential and limits.

"Reading" the Environment

When Amelia arrived, the teachers were helping children choose by using their Classroom Manager's Rules: If a child doesn't know what she wants to do, give her two choices. If she can't choose between them, choose for her. The key to self-discipline in the MELC was this process of individually settling children into activities they chose. Amelia helped the teachers expand the technique by engaging children in rule-making, in analyzing the environment and all its potential.

First, teachers thought through the limits themselves: How many chairs will fit here? How many children will fit at this table? They reorganized the space if they thought limits needed to change or be clearer. Then they discussed each aspect of the environment with one small group at a time, telling children the story of each area, teaching them to read the story, making explicit connections among organization, rule, and choice. For example, in the Communication Center: "There are four chairs here. How many children do you think can be here?" Area by area they negotiated: "How many can play here? Is there enough space? What do you think?" Amelia explained that studying children's choices is the basis for negotiating with them. So the teachers wrote down children's answers to discuss among themselves, then to discuss again with the children, initiating situations that, as Carlina said, use conflict to drive growth. Teachers did this with each different material as well as each area, stimulating children's ideas, nurturing hypotheses of what they might do, determining children's rights, negotiating until they reached a consensus.

Trying New Things

If the same child always went to a particular area, the teachers tried to understand why by discussing with the child the reasons for his choice. The purpose was not for the children to diversify their interests, although that might happen, but to help them choose more thoughtfully by understanding their own motives. Amelia noticed that five children always used concentration cards. At full-group meeting she questioned them: Why had they chosen the cards? What made them notice them? What did they like about them? She then invited two of the five to use the cards with two younger children. This made the older children reflective about their choice and provided a new reason to use the cards.

Choosing to Draw

Teachers noticed that Terrell rarely chose to draw, resisting if asked. In October a small group had visited the White House where their drawings of cars were exhibited at a press conference on clean cars of the future. This huge experience had stimulated Terrell to draw beautiful cars. But a month later, in November 1993, when teachers invited the children to the Studio to draw animals they were discussing, Terrell, obstinate and completely stuck, refused to try. Amelia saw the conflict between Jennifer, asking him to draw, and Terrell, saying, "I can't. I don't want to." She jumped in: "Are you so certain? I remember something," and showed him his earlier drawing: "Here's your beautiful car." Terrell answered, "Cars are different. Animals are hard." Amelia asked, "Can you try?"

Alone together they went to the Communication Center. He drew several animals, which Jennifer greatly admired. From then on Terrell chose to draw spontaneously (see Figure 7.3).

Children in Reggio choose to draw all the time; if they've been in an infant center, they draw before they are 3. In the MELC it wasn't easy to start because the children had no prior experience. MELC Day visitors asked if we ever had a child who never chose to draw. Yes! Alonzo never drew. Jennifer explained that, initially, teachers had not asked children to draw enough; materials had stayed in one area; quantities were limited, and therefore their appeal diminished. The first change was putting pencils and markers in many areas; then they encouraged children to move them from area to area and provided increasingly more drawing materials. Teachers also made a concerted effort to ask children to draw on every possible occasion. Now drawing occurred everywhere—on the floor, on clipboards, with pencils, with markers or fine point pens, in an atmosphere where drawing was fun and they drew things they loved, like the turtle or Coco. By June 1995 children asked to draw all the time and when teachers asked, "Do you want to draw?" they heard a resounding Yes!

Drawing was emphasized as a powerful means of communication, different from speech because in speaking one can gloss over detail whereas in drawing one cannot. For example, the child who expressed the theory that trains were powered by steam could say, "The steam makes it go," and no one would know if he understood how. The process of drawing would cause him to show what he understood about the relationship between steam and wheels.

Choosing Whom to Involve

The teachers gradually learned how to choose children for groups. For example, they hoped older children would help new children master a new, stretchy, hard-to-use glue. Concurrently, they were exploring all the materials in the Communication Center because many new students needed to learn both about the materials and the rule that only four could be there at once (only four chairs fit!). And a panel, Surprises for New Children, had just been mounted. Simultaneously, a group was working with Genet, making gifts for Amelia's children in Reggio.

Through careful consideration of the children, the teachers created an intersection among these particular activities. First, they considered which children were

FIGURE 7.3. Terrell's Cat. (Drawing)

most competent with the glue and with the area, and best able to help new children make gifts, and especially interested in the new panel. They chose the four children who fit all these criteria to form the group. Other activities would have different criteria and therefore a different group would emerge from the teachers' consideration. Enormous thought went into forming groups for particular activities.

On an MELC Day in June 1994, Genet explained how teachers analyzed children's interest in a project. First, they *surmised* who might be interested, but couldn't be sure until they approached the children. A child might decide to join; if not, the teachers would ask why. Not joining was OK, and by asking, the teachers learned more about her preferences. In 1992 Malaguzzi told the visiting delegation to Reggio: "An environment for children is a rich network of possible situations in which an adult envisions relationships that will facilitate children's work."

The words "envisions relationships" sprang to life in the process of choosing. Tiziana would say to "contaminate" children through contact with one another's interests (Reggio Conference, June 1994). Amelia helped us understand what that meant.

Modeling How to Choose

Teachers negotiated together in children's presence. As children heard them voicing opinions, reaching consensus, they also learned to do so, "stealing," as Malaguzzi said, adults' ways of working together:

> Even if children are naturally endowed with the art of making friends or acting as teachers among their peers, they do not improve this art by means of instinct or books. They steal and interpret patterns from adult teachers; . . . the more . . . teachers know how to work, discuss, think, and research together, the more children get. (Malaguzzi & Filippini, 1991, p. 17)

Teachers learned to help a child who refused a particular activity by observing and discussing the child's choices among themselves, then with the child. Each teacher had different insights about the nature of each child's preferences. They helped children overcome their reluctance in many ways: analyzing prior work, enriching the environment, encouraging relationships among the children, negotiating with a child, forging connections among activities going on simultaneously, even if the activities seemed disconnected. For example, if a child loved the computer but hated drawing, a teacher could put pencils and paper on the computer table and ask the child to draw what she saw on the screen. If she refused, the teacher could bring a friend who liked drawing to the task, or ask the child to make the drawing because it was needed in the Studio. Such techniques, alone or in combination, usually enticed a reluctant child.

Amelia told MELC Day participants in June 1993: "The adult's role is to make a choice, take a risk! No one taught me how to make good choices; I had to try myself in order to learn. If a child has something in mind and can give us a reason, it's OK."

Metacognition means awareness of one's own thinking processes and understanding that others have unique perspectives that may differ. One way metacognition develops is when a child talks with other children or with teachers about what he's thinking as he chooses. When children choose and observe others choosing, they develop a consciousness of their own minds.

WHAT WE LEARNED

An especially hard change had been for the teachers to learn how to listen. What were the children really saying? Which of their ideas had potential to engage them in rich work? What was their *driving* remark, the one to pursue in a project, or to represent in a panel?

As hard as it was to learn to detect meaning in children's remarks, however, it was harder to learn to listen to one another, to ask for help, to say to colleagues,

"I don't understand what I am doing." How could Genet admit she did not know how to have a conversation with a child? How could Jennifer learn to say what was on her mind when it could sound critical of a colleague? How could Sonya accept criticism from people she saw every day? How could Wendy, whose background was so different, trust the others? Had they understood in spring 1992 that being vulnerable was essential to adapting the Reggio approach, they might not have proceeded, the fear of exposure killing the desire for change.

Some things, like "stealing time," they learned through Amelia's pushing for change; some, like facing criticism, through her coaching. Others, like the process of planning for the unexpected, they learned through the brute force of attempt after attempt. The richness families bring to a program they learned by reexamining their beliefs through long discussions over many months. Initiating and sustaining small-group work and documenting experiences they learned working side-by-side with Amelia. Most difficult was learning to use their vulnerability as a catalyst for change. It took a long time for strong, different women to speak openly together.

Among our Italian colleagues it appeared that argument began discussion; in America argument ends discussion because in our culture many view argument as impolite. Gradually, Amelia helped the teachers learn how to state their opinions, explain their choices, and be receptive to better choices; how to be confrontational without being destructive; how to disagree without triggering rancor; how to accept criticism without being defensive; how to acknowledge mistakes without making excuses or blaming. It was a huge breakthrough when they finally began to realize the value of others' perspectives, that criticism can strengthen one's own performance. Through long hours of discussion and individual soul-searching they had learned to yield individual control to group process. Their passion for working with children and desire to work with economically at-risk families had assuaged them through the difficult process.

By year-end, the teachers could keep time fluid, plan for the spontaneous, and embrace the unexpected. They could engage in heated exchanges and passionate disputes. They saw the children's growth, the wealth of new panels, and visitors' awe. And, during the accreditation process when the examiners probed their feelings, their answers showed how much they had learned to trust one another.

CHAPTER 8

A Path to Literacy

*Writers may not be . . . sensitive or talented in any unusual sense. They are simply
engaged in sustained use of a skill we all have.*

William Stafford, *Writing the Australian Crawl*

In school year 1993–94 MELC parents expressed concerns about reading and writing. This coincided with a national push for accountability in education. A decade had elapsed since the U.S. National Commission on Excellence in Education (1983) issued a report alleging that America's schools were failing. One result of the report was increased pressure for test scores to meet national norms; another was testing at younger ages, including kindergarten. In the name of readiness, an agenda developed for what children must know when they begin first grade and what kindergarten must teach. The era of free play and incidental academic content was over. From the early 1980s, attitudes shifted, imposing prescribed lessons on increasingly younger children. A politically based accountability movement emphasizing test scores began in earnest.

Our parents' concerns reflected that mood. However, we were experiencing just the beginning of social as well as political changes: In 1970, 61% of families had stay-at-home mothers; by 2002, 79% of mothers were employed (AFL-CIO). As the twenty-first century began, this thrust public schools into preschool education with two effects: First, grade-school work was pushed into kindergarten and preschool; and second, high-stakes testing, even for Head Start, became the norm. A comment by the superintendent of a large public school system typifies the attitude: "Nap time needs to go away. . . . we need to get rid of all the baby school stuff they used to do" (Trejos, 2004, p. A01). From the perspective of young children's development, it is a dangerous movement with great potential harm.

Our parents' concerns were early harbingers of the soon-to-shift attitudes. In response, we increased our language activities, taking care to explain them to parents, including the purpose for using symbols and the relevance of the Studio and projects in acquiring literacy. These are the subjects of this chapter.

AN ANXIOUS TIME

In October 1993 several parents reported that first-grade teachers were questioning whether their older children, former MELC students, were adequately prepared. Parents' concerns aroused teachers' concerns. On November 1, 1993, the teachers sent me a memo, "Reading and Writing":

Today a parent called whose child is now in first grade and is having some problems. Unfortunately her situation is not one of a kind.

Another child is doing okay in reading, but having trouble recognizing numbers over 20. The teacher gave parents a list of what children should know when they begin school. The mother was surprised there was so much and claimed we never covered some of it.

Another child had to be tested to get into first grade and was admitted reluctantly. The teacher feels the child should know how to read more.

Another child doesn't know how to write well enough; this is causing quite a bit of stress. The mother is very concerned, especially with a sibling in our program.

Another, her aunt says, is doing OK. However, the child doesn't like school and wants to come back to us.

In response to parents' concerns, Wendy and Sonya met with all former MELC children's first-grade teachers to explain our program. As a staff we reviewed our entire approach to literacy.

The MELC's Approach to Literacy

By far our most prevalent activities involved use of the English language; there were over a dozen distinct activities to build literacy, including regular use of Montessori Sandpaper Letters and Movable Alphabet, time-proven materials with which writing is taught as a prelude to reading. In response to parents' concerns, we focused extra attention on all language activities, especially conversation, which builds prereading skills, teaching children through practice how the language works.

Conversations. Records for the first 8 weeks alone note 53 conversations during full-class meetings. Although lots of talk occurred on the fly, it was only considered a conversation if a focused, extended exchange of ideas occurred. Conversations were planned or spontaneous, spurred by teachers' hypotheses, by what children brought from home, by any question or remark, by a book, something new in the classroom, the weather, or yesterday's field trip. Anything!

Sonya orchestrated conversations well, intuitively paying the speaker respect, insisting firmly that everyone pay attention. Gradually, the other teachers learned these skills. The adults' behavior set the tone: total engagement, intent concentration; eyes did not wander; heads never drifted from the speaker. They expected the same from the children. Their insistence that each child focus, coupled with their own bearing, taught the children to listen to the speaker, a valuable lesson in paying attention. Because teachers' own demeanor and their expectations for children's behavior were entirely consistent, conversations grew in length—one minute, then 10, eventually half an hour—becoming a mainstay of full-group meetings, with the children absorbed and not restless. The effect was reciprocal: Speakers were encouraged to speak; listeners became engaged in the ideas. Use of the English language—complete thoughts, full sentences, expanding vocabulary—flowered as a result.

Conversations also grew in scope. There were seven reports-back in Amelia's first 5 weeks, accorded the same respect as conversations. By November, conversations covered as many as five topics in one full-group meeting: the meeting's purpose, favorite moments at the fire station, new students' feelings, what to do for new friends, and a report-back on a project. Teachers informed parents of the emphasis on conversation, explaining how it increases vocabulary, builds grammatical structure, fosters articulate speech, introduces new ideas, and develops practice in following a train of thought—all essential prerequisites for reading and writing. When visitors expressed surprise at the children's articulateness, teachers credited the emphasis on conversation.

Books. Books were read frequently: during full-group meetings, in small groups, and in one-on-one sessions between teacher and child or child and child, including books the children wrote with their teachers. The Big Room contained a good-sized library and books were available everywhere throughout the school. Books of interest to families were in the Parent Room. Children made frequent trips to the public library, borrowing books for the classroom or doing project research, not only in children's books, but tapping the full library for specific images or information. Teachers made additional space so more books could be immediately accessible, in the Studio, the Lab, alongside maps and other materials, anywhere a book with rich images related to a particular material. They increased books-on-tape in the listening area. Book Sharing (described in Chapter 3) remained vital. Teachers discussed with parents how to increase the effective use of books at home.

Letters. Teachers put more focus on letters, asking families to collect letters, sorting them with the children, adding jars of letters to the Big Room and Communication Center, using them to read and write. Wendy used the Sandpaper Letters and Movable Alphabet more frequently. Amelia intensified the amount of message writing between school and home, among children, and whenever there might be cause for a message. A huge traffic in messages was occasioned by Amelia's bringing gifts made by the La Villetta children. Like hounds, the teachers became keen detectors of any glimmer of a possible reason for message writing. Staff wrote more in front of the children and expanded the amount of children's writing on messages home. The teachers described these activities at parent meetings.

The Reading Conundrum

Did the emphasis on literacy allay parents' concerns? It did somewhat, as in ensuing months the staff described how language experiences were infused through every activity. But parents never feel assured in a culture where test scores are the proof that children have learned and school funding is legislatively tied to test scores. Did the staff's increased emphasis on literacy make a difference in the children's later school performance? We don't know; we had neither time to collect information to answer this question nor funds to conduct research with methods like control groups and statistical analysis.

When questioned about what impact their practices have on children's performance in later grades, Reggio educators say the issue is irrelevant to their concerns and exclaim, "Just look at how our town functions if you want to see our results!" Reggio Emilia is renowned in the business world for its collaborative manufacturing practices, and in government circles for its citizen's participatory budgeting practices. I doubt that Americans would have the patience to wait decades for results of preschool practices to emerge. There are no easy answers for the reading conundrum in which our culture is caught.

Wendy told parents how Alonzo, who had used blocks for 6 months, had counted, sorted, categorized, organized, arranged—essential initial skills for mastering reading, writing, and arithmetic. She said, "As teachers, we have to step back! Children get to reading and writing when they are ready if these kinds of preparation are always taking place." Today, as preset kindergarten and preschool curricula increasingly dominate early school experience, children are required to sit still and be quiet, listening for long periods while teachers "teach" language skills. At the age when children should acquire language skills actively by using them, they are instead silenced. If we wanted to assure later language failure, the proscribed lessons, which eliminate talking, would be an ideal way to do so. When practices that are inimical to language development are coupled with the long hours children spend silently watching television, it is a double prescription for language failure.

Gardner (1983) says that children who are not language performers have other innate strengths, like music, movement, or math. As a parent, I would observe my child carefully and feed his strengths. As a teacher, I would advise parents: significantly increase the amount of conversation. Turn off the TV, read lots of books, discuss them. Young children are capable of long, serious discussion.

And for children who have no one to observe? to converse with? to turn off the TV? or to read books? These are problems. As the century turned, policy makers said testing was the answer. Yet, there are well-researched cases against excessive testing (Gardner, 2000; Sacks, 1999). Literacy problems could be better solved by a national effort to mentor more and test less.

SYMBOLS AND LITERACY

In the 1990s the use of symbols in Reggio schools was unique. Every child had her own symbol, which teachers used in dozens of specific ways throughout each school. Using symbols in a preschool recognizes the powerful relationship humans have had with symbols in many prehistoric cultures. They are a special kind of writing from 20,000 years ago, predating alphabets by millennia. From humans' earliest marks on cave walls, our species has been symbol makers. The connection with reading is that both symbols and words represent ideas. Babies grasp this powerful fact when, from 12 to 18 months, they begin using words intentionally.

Choosing Symbols

On their first visit to the MELC, every new family and their child chose a symbol. From source books with thousands of symbols in the public domain, the MELC selected over 600 for a book that became the class "Symbol Dictionary," used by each incoming family. It never failed to provide a symbol that excited a child. Some represented familiar things, like animals or vehicles; others were geometric forms; some were emblems or insignia; others represented different cultures, such as African American or Native American. Still others were objects children love—cats, trains, toys—or excited innate attraction to aesthetic forms with pleasing lines—snowflakes, crosses. The children's pleasure made the teachers' effort worthwhile—making masters, maintaining storage systems, affixing, copying. Such preparation and care, essential in Reggio practices, became a way of life in the MELC.

A child and parent might differ in their choice, but the process of selecting a symbol was a strong motive to resolve argument. Teachers who observed found clues to a child's behavior and home relationships, learned how families handled conflict, and thereby enlarged their own repertoire of ways to resolve disputes. Selecting a symbol calmed anxious feelings, refocusing the moment from separation to inclusion, as parent and child did something essential to the school, alleviating fear of the new environment through involvement in a riveting experience.

When a symbol was selected and before a child's first day in school, teachers put a copy in the Greeting Room under the child's photo; on his attendance marker, mailbox, portfolio, Book Sharing bag, and bathroom drawer; and wherever symbols were used in systems, like the attendance board, the birthday calendar, and the Lunchtime Helper panel. Thus, on their child's first day, parents saw their choice valued. Children saw immediately where to put possessions, and felt a sense of belonging. Name, photo, symbol appeared so often, used in so many ways, it became part of a child's context, a familiar reference also reflecting his family. Because children kept the same symbol throughout their school years, symbols came to represent them.

Teachers might decide that, if someone selected a butterfly, no one else could, even if the butterflies differed (see Figure 8.1). Or, teachers might encourage children to select any symbol regardless. Whichever path teachers chose, consistency was important. Children have a strong sense of justice and long memories! If two or three did select butterflies, it offered an opportunity for conversation: How would we know which belongs to each child? What details distinguish one from another? In nature, within one species there are different breeds; how does each know its own kind? Such conversations involved concepts like subtlety, similarity, camouflage, perception, conflict. Symbols caused children and families to observe and communicate, two important processes in reading and writing.

Using Symbols

Children talked about their symbols both spontaneously and in teacher-initiated conversations. They described, classified, drew, and played games with them, invented stories about them, used them on messages. Early in 1993–94, symbols were used in five places, by year-end in over 20, evidence of teachers' refining the environment. Because uses for symbols stemmed from real needs, children needed to "read" the symbols: Whose is this? Who is here today? Whose birthdays are this month? Who are lunch helpers? In this system children agreed who would help that month, then inserted chosen helpers' name, symbol, photo tags into holders on the lunch calendar, two for each day. Tags enabled children themselves to see whose turn it was. The system familiarized them with how calendars work.

Through many experiences children came to value symbols and, since symbols represented them, to realize they were valued. While children differed in when they remembered which symbol stood for whom, eventually all did. As they

FIGURE 8.1. Butterfly symbols express the same idea differently.

observed, discriminated, memorized, and manipulated symbols, children acquired power over them. Studies of *locus of control*—a person's perception of whether he controls his world or it controls him—show that a person is stronger—cognitively, socially, emotionally—if he feels in control. Symbols included the kinds of icons used extensively for computers and signage, two areas in which symbols are short-hand for entire ideas, thus preparing children to use these dominant communication systems.

Understanding Abstraction

Symbols are more abstract than physical objects, less so than written words. An important step for a prereader is to make the connection between something real, like an object or action, and something abstract, like a symbol or word. "Reading" symbols makes this connection. Children learn that symbols represent a person, object, action, or idea. Because symbols are a step toward understanding the significance of writing, they are important on the journey to literacy.

Other educators have long recognized how magical it is for young children to grasp the purpose of reading and writing: "Written language was understood by children . . . as another way of expressing themselves, another form of spoken language . . . to be transmitted directly from one person to another" (Montessori, 1936/1965, p.151). In Montessori schools children first read little slips of paper. The teacher writes a slip in front of the child, then folds or rolls it, and hands it to her with great ceremony: *Open the window,* and off she runs to do so. *Give her a kiss. Bring him the pen,* messages revealing writing's power to command, caress, or summon. "First words must have intense meaning for a child. They must be part of his being" (Ashton-Warner, 1963, p. 30). Today's psychologists confirm this, knowing that even babies have abstract and concrete internal representations of language.

Symbols in the MELC were important beyond purposes of identification. They were used to communicate, both meaning (this is Tamika's) and intent (I want to write to my friends). Thus symbols abounded in the Communication Center, where containers held dozens of every child's symbol, ready to paste on messages children constantly sent via each other's mailboxes (see Figure 8.2). Malaguzzi had explained the mailboxes to our Reggio delegation in March 1992:

> Children are hungry to make friends, and it's not easy. They restlessly seek to talk, discuss, negotiate. When we began to understand this, we created a honeycomb of boxes so each child could receive messages or presents from the others. We also agreed with the families to help with the traffic created by messages and friendship gifts.
>
> Early each morning, children go to their box to see what is there. . . . If you could see the evolution of these gifts—at first a button from mother's dress or a bead from mother's necklace, a piece of paper, or candy. By the time they are 5 they have learned to write without even being taught because they see others write. They learn in order to send the messages. Communication is a natural process in our schools.

FIGURE 8.2. Children checked their mailboxes for messages several times a day. (Communication Center)

Rationale

The roots of literacy lie in infancy. Infants stare fixedly at facial features and respond differently to a smile than to a grimace. They are especially sensitive to images with sharp contrast at the edges. Vision is ultimately complex, yet one of the most researched brain functions. To develop, the visual system requires an external stimulus or input, highly specialized receptors in the brain, and interpretation by other highly specialized brain cells, which change as they respond, thereby developing. This process is certain to occur since humans are born with a propensity to seek visual stimulation (Damasio, 1994; Ornstein & Thompson, 1984). The Nobel Prize of 1981 for work by David Hubel and Torsten Wiesel showed that in kittens total deprivation of visual stimulation at a specific period in infancy can result in permanent blindness (Cool, 1996).

Research on vision has implications for the kind and amounts of visual stimulation that infant centers and preschools should provide. In making symbols so important, Reggio educators tapped into a powerful historical, cultural, and biological force. That is not surprising. Part of Reggio schools' effectiveness is that their creators have powerful intuition about young children and are masters at translating their intuition into intentional practices.

THE STUDIO'S CONNECTION

Reggio educators see connections many of us might miss, so, if pressed, could probably make a strong case for how Studio activities bear on reading and writing. However, this is not their focus. In contrast, our culture puts enormous emphasis on early acquisition of literacy skills. Therefore, in addressing parents' concerns the MELC staff laid the template of reading and writing readiness on Studio activities to help parents see how these activities prepare children to read and write, directly or indirectly.

Two central acts in reading are decoding letter sequences into a sound pattern that is recognizable as a word (p-e-t = pet) and understanding the meaning of words (When I pet Coco, he purrs). Two central acts in writing are wielding a writing implement skillfully and organizing what one wants to say in logical sequence. We tried to help parents understand that these are extremely complex acts, made up of multitudes of separate skills. We tried to show how the kinds of experiences that abounded in the MELC related to literacy skills—engagement with the meaning of words through books, conversation, and projects; familiarity with sequencing through the process of doing projects; use of materials and tools requiring increasingly precise hand movements. We explained how keeping young children seated at prescribed workbook-like tasks can kill their love of learning; how urging them to explore all the school's books would help them see books as valuable; how the search through books for particular information could motivate them to read. We showed parents the intriguing writing materials and explained how all the different ways we used writing could motivate children to write. We described research on the importance of motivation in learning to read and write, that a child's own desire is a more effective spur than stars or candy. We demonstrated the specific materials we used to teach letters and numbers, explaining that we generally used them one-on-one, teacher to child, targeting each lesson to one individual child's level. We made sure parents understood that young children must learn in ways compatible with their need to move, talk, laugh, and relate to others, and that Studio activities enabled them to do so. We explained that children learn to concentrate by continuing an activity for as long as they remain interested, that an individual child's attention span, not a preplanned lesson, should dictate when to stop because young children learn to concentrate by concentrating. Gradually parents began to see how Studio activities related to their concerns about literacy.

Initial Studio Activities

In June 1993 the Studio reflected Jennifer's first attempts: Intriguing materials—carefully classified by size, color, and texture—filled glass jars that covered tall storage shelves. Many came from families: bits and pieces of ribbon, string, buttons, broken jewelry, bottle tops—the detritus of daily life. A variety of empty jars waited for more. Cardboard and Styrofoam, which abound in American homes, were organized in neat stacks by size, shape, color, and thickness. So was evidence of fall and various holidays. Amazed at the wealth, visitors were astonished to learn that materials came from children's homes. Children learned to use them to express their ideas and intentions.

Self-Portraits. Four children's work hung under the title "Different Selves." Each had carefully examined her face in a mirror and made six self-portraits (see Figure 8.3) alongside a color photo in —words; textures; tempera paint; #2 pencil; fine-line black marker; pastel on black paper. Quatesha said: "I did all of these, I did a thousand. No, just one, two, three, four, five, six. The hair looks like mine, eyebrows and everything. I covered up the eyes and the nose on the painting." Jennifer noted: "I asked Quatesha why it is important to look at, write about, and draw ourselves. She replied, 'Because it's beautiful.'"

First Mobile. The Lemon Tree project began on March 26, 1993, the provocation being three lemons Jennifer hung from the ceiling to pique interest, she thought, in making a mural of fruit and vegetables for the house. Instead, in a project spanning several days, children decided to make life-size papier mâché lemons. By April 16, the lemons and other objects, including transparent bags with lightweight yellow objects, yellow paper and gels in varied shapes, and yellow items brought from home, were ready to attach to a tree limb, in all a striking effect. The project built manual dexterity and visual and spatial awareness.

Other Works. A panel over the sink displayed the results of investigating circular objects. A large mosaic near the mirrors contained the results, in words and images, of several days' investigation of watercolor. Tentative shapes displayed on shelves marked beginning works in clay. Working in the Studio inculcated an attitude: If I want to make something, I am competent and can do so in many different ways, an attitude that could transfer to many different situations.

The question of *transfer*—whether a skill gained in one area transfers to another that is significantly different—is worth considering. Research suggests that if teachers make children aware of the connections between seemingly disparate ideas or activities as they are engaged in an activity, they will learn to make connections

FIGURE 8.3. Three children made their self-portraits in six different media. (Studio)

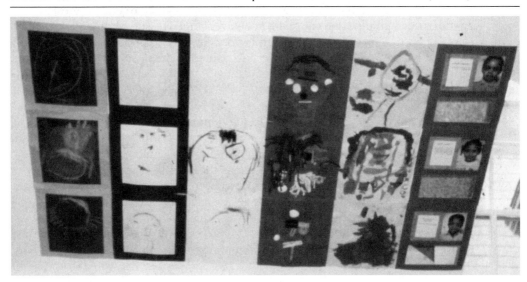

themselves. "[When] students learned the knowledge in the context of problem-solving tasks, the knowledge is better organized in their minds for later problem solving" (Perkins, 1992, p. 127). Work in the Studio frequently required children to acquire specific knowledge in order to solve problems. What Reggio educators call "translating from one language to another" is an example of transfer.

Jennifer believes art *is* the curriculum. But in September 1993 she did not know how to tie the Studio into the MELC's other activities: "On my first day with Amelia I felt absolutely isolated." A year later she described how her outlook had changed:

> Now I understand that I am the resource to help the children use a hundred languages, to translate from language to language.
> Everything that goes on in the Studio is a link to things happening elsewhere in the school and also a link between school and home.

Progress in Studio Activities

Visitors marveled at creations in paint, ink, wire, clay, paper, fiber, and other materials. Some resulted from collaboration among children, others from one child's effort. Some visitors left thinking the school had an extraordinary art program. Although beautiful art was produced, its production was not the goal. The goal was to confront children with a great variety of ways to express themselves, then use their expressions—through teachers' careful listening and observation—to help them express themselves ever more clearly. That is, if a teacher can see what a child is thinking, the teacher can engage in a more responsive dialogue with the child. Cognitive scientist Rochel Gelman studies young children's thinking:

> Ways of thinking, doing, and communicating about the world are at the heart of scientific enterprise. Thinking includes predicting and checking. Doing includes observing, comparing, contrasting, quantifying. Communicating includes recording and sharing findings with others. If children are offered the opportunity to do these things rather than memorizing facts, we give them a learning environment in which scientific minds can, and will, develop. (personal communication, December 2004)

In the MELC and Reggio schools the goal is not art for art's sake, but art for thinking's sake, in science, math, language, and all other domains. Beautiful art is a by-product.

In the Studio, links are forged among materials, tools, and children's skills, thoughts, and feelings. The children learn both how to use their hands to make their ideas tangible and how materials can represent their feelings. For example, at Diana School in Reggio Emilia, children had used clay to express how it felt to be caught in the swell of a crowd of people; their figures, which they massed in a crowd on the huge table, pushed against one another. Some figures' facial expressions conveyed fear of claustrophobia; others conveyed glee at being in a crowd. Similarly, in the MELC, children would comment on feelings: "I'm beautiful." "The turtle's head is hiding because it scared." "Coco don't like it when its eyes are poked." "It made me angry [when the water was polluted]."

Research supports Reggio educators' recognition of the link between feeling and thinking:

> Feelings are just as cognitive as any other perceptual image, and just as dependent on cerebral-cortex processing. . . . What makes [feelings] different is that they are first and foremost about the body, that they offer us the cognition of our visceral and musculoskeletal state. (Damasio, 1994, p. 159)

By June 1994 the Studio had hardly a bare surface; children's work covered window panes, shelves, and walls. Jennifer said it "reflected the process of choosing particular materials and the many different languages." A top shelf held three small weavings on looms made of wire, cardboard, or string. A lower shelf held cardboard and collage projects. The wall above had paper sculptures—some rolled, others accordion-folded; some cut in strips, zigzags, or wavy lines, some decorated with colored markers, others with pencil. One panel had still-life drawings of the Christmas cactus. Affixed to another were 43 small, differently shaped objects, wrapped in various papers (see Figure 8.4). A third panel had reliefs—foil pressed over collages of three-dimensional objects, then inked. A fourth had collages of fall objects, pasted inside small "found" (jewelry) boxes. Tempera paintings, not yet stored in children's portfolios, hung on easels. On one shelf Coco reclined in a remarkably lifelike clay sculpture. On another, two clay figures stood, three-dimensional portraits of the body, an exercise Amelia suggested to improve Jennifer's observation skills. Documentation of the project titled "Alonzo's Dinosaur" hung over the mirrors. The work proclaimed what had occurred in the Studio—a wealth of experience using a great variety of materials and many new techniques, reflecting Jennifer's growing understanding of her role and the children's increasing competence in "languages."

Further Evidence of Growth

As each of 4 successive years began, the teachers responded to children's excitement about changes occurring outside by doing a project called Fall. Looking across these years, we can see the teachers' developing skills.

1992-93. A project that started outside quickly came into the Studio. Jennifer explained:

> The children were bringing in signs of fall, things they found
> outside, with questions about what was changing. As we listened,
> trying to decide what they were saying, we found they were espe-
> cially interested in color. In small groups we did weavings and
> collage [using fall objects]. The class visited the Arboretum and ran
> through the leaves. Teachers brought leaves here to brainstorm how
> to help children express themselves using the leaves.

One outcome was a thick carpet of ginkgo leaves—intensely yellow in fall—which teachers placed in the kaleidoscope. Children who crawled inside saw their reflection engulfed in utter yellowness.

FIGURE 8.4. The children wrapped 43 objects in different kinds of paper. (Studio)

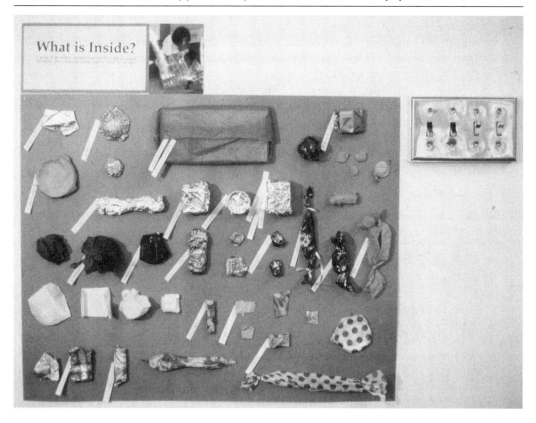

1993-94. Fall activities were similar, but extended into more media, not only weavings and collage but also rubbings, prints, clay impressions, and drawings.

1994-95. The project became richer, expanding to include other seasons. Responding to Giovanni's provocation to work "Big," teachers hung a huge tree limb horizontally, close to the ceiling, parallel to the floor, its branches trailing down, and attached lengths of chicken wire to enhance the verticality. *Mobilesque* was Jennifer's word. They hung evidence of fall from the branches, and wove objects through the wire. As the seasons changed, children modified the branches' appearance and teachers documented each stage to make a permanent record. Children wrote a poem for each season and, echoing the big tree, made collages in other scales, on wire fastened to smaller pieces of branches or in boxes. Together teachers and children transformed natural objects into other, entirely different things, like a seed pod into a dragonfly. Jennifer divided a huge cardboard into squares to make a grid; in each cell a different medium represented fall—leaf prints, watercolor, drawings, collage, natural materials, words—past activities now integrated in a complex tapestry. As seasons changed, so did materials, becoming an exploration: materials through the seasons.

1995-96. Investigations took other directions. From the museum's highest balcony, children dropped various objects, including leaves, and drew their paths as they fell—zigzags, flats, and angles. Children animated a leaf's fall in the video studio. To represent the space through which leaves fall, Jennifer and the children bent chicken wire into a zigzag shape, following the pattern in their drawings; the form reached from floor to ceiling. In it they wove feathers, papers, and fabrics to represent falling leaves' paths (see Figure 8.5). Jennifer said it helped her learn about metaphor: she realized that when one thing stands for another, it need not be a literal representation.

FIGURE 8.5. The children represented the path of falling leaves with various materials in a large wire sculpture. (Studio)

As Jennifer and the Studio matured, so did the depth of the experiences. In addition to any direct or indirect preparation for reading and writing, Studio activities helped children learn to approach complex tasks, to assess what tools and materials they needed, to engage others collaboratively, to focus and sustain their attention, and to use many different media to express their thoughts and feelings, all essential literacy skills.

Our culture seems to focus on literacy in early education to the exclusion of many other skills. While there is no denying the connection between literacy and later success in school, there is reason to question the effectiveness of our means of achieving literacy. Because young children value what they see others do, especially their parents, it raises the questions of whether our children see us read enough and whether our time spent reading to them is sufficiently frequent to inculcate a love of reading. If we had to credit any single source at the MELC for the children's increasing literacy skills, it would be documentation that connected children to words in the most powerful way—reading stories about themselves; this in turn connected their parents to the school as the children, with increasing skill, "read" them the stories.

CHAPTER 9

Materials, Projects, and Documentation

Every time we invest attention in an idea, a written word, a spectacle, the texture of the future is changed, even if in microscopic ways. . . . These small choices, these trivial decisions, have as much weight in the long run as all of Napoleon's wars.
                              Mihaly Csikszentmihalyi, *The Evolving Self*

In a system anything you do affects everything else. In the classroom there is a relationship between each Reggio practice and every other one. In this chapter I explore the relationship among materials, documentation, and projects.

MATERIALS

Reggio educators use materials as a vehicle for children ultimately to speak fluently in a hundred languages. This means honing many skills along dimensions of human capacity that vary enormously. The teachers consider this serious work and give it abundant time. Children become familiar with materials' potential, make big plans for using them, and anticipate the fun they'll have. Meantime, bonds between families and school strengthen as parents see the care paid to materials they send from home.

A Hundred Tiny Doors

The large panes on the bottom rows of the Studio's windows displayed children's collage-like work—dozens of tiny objects glued on specially prepared paper. The paper had the weight of bond, so it was substantial, and the transparency of onion skin, so it was translucent. When finished collages were mounted on the panes, light shining through made the objects look like they were floating. Because all the panes were covered, they immediately drew attention. You felt you were looking at miniature scenes through dozens of doors.

The "doors" resulted from teachers' careful preparation of the papers. First, they cut the bond-weight paper to the pane's exact size. Then, in each piece, they cut rows of rectangular flaps, 35 per paper, each the same size, about 3 cm × 3.5 cm. Because the flaps were cut on only three sides and the attached side was creased, they stood upright, looking like rows of small, open doors. A piece of paper with doors was glued onto a backing of clear acetate in the exact size. Children chose objects to glue "through" the doors onto the acetate behind. Objects varied in color, size, shape, texture, opacity, reflectivity, abstractness, and every other attribute. For example: sequins, bugle beads, scraps of theater gel, mini–paper clips, assorted beads and buttons, bits of tinsel, foils, shiny fabric, chips of iridescent shells, tiny pebbles, grains of rice, tips of twigs.

Method. Because finished work would be displayed with light shining through, to see the effect of light as they worked, children created the collages on the light table. Along the back stood small containers, each holding a different kind of object, and bottles of transparent dressmaker's glue. At the front were the specially prepared papers, two because only two children could fit side by side. The activity involved gluing at least one object in each door, until all the doors were full (see Figure 9.1). Each child who chose the activity completed a paper, alone or with friends.

Effect. Each paper was awesome, like those Easter eggs grandly decorated with colored sugar, into which one peers to see a mesmerizing scene transporting the viewer to its miniature world. While scenes in the eggs are realistic, scenes through the doors were abstract. Filling all the spaces required persistence, dexterity (such tiny objects, such sticky glue!), and determination. The effect was enhanced by the design's regularity, by each paper's covering a pane, and by all bottom panes being covered. Most engaging were the multitude and variety of objects, overall the same, yet each a distinct bit.

FIGURE 9.1. *A Hundred Tiny Doors* on all the bottom window panes. (Studio)

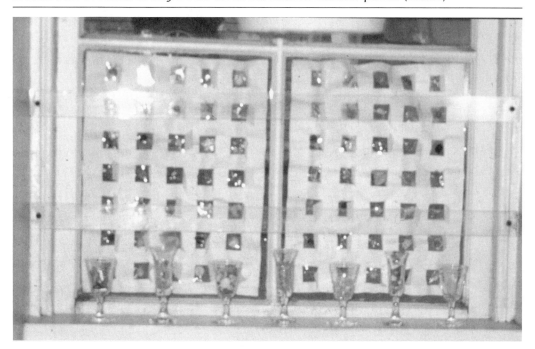

Outcome. Families supplied many of the objects, saw the work in progress, and viewed the project on video. Teachers provoked the activity, laboriously prepared the papers, and made the video. Children honed their skill in handling tiny objects and using glue, and experienced the satisfaction of completing a big project. Families especially liked the video. Everyone—children, teachers, parents, visitors—was awed by the effect. The admiration built the children's self-esteem, reinforcing their self-confidence.

A Theory in Practice. Reuven Feuerstein's theory of the Mediated Learning Experience (MLE; see Chapter 3) highlights the role of a mediator (parent, teacher, other adult, or child) as the essential link that determines the impact of a learning experience (Feuerstein et al., 1991). MLE is compatible with Reggio practices, in which the collaboration between teacher and child is the mediating factor in the learning experience.

Among MLE's many characteristics, purpose, meaning, intent, and transcendent meaning are of paramount importance in focusing a child's attention. If analyzed in MLE terms, the doors project had evident *purpose*—make something beautiful for the classroom; clear *meaning*—materials look different with light behind them; and obvious *intent*—fill all the spaces. It had rich *transcendent meanings*—our work together makes a greater statement than any single piece; natural and artificial light vary; light affects materials differently; I can use light as a medium.

The hypotheses were that the task would motivate children to complete a large undertaking; that parents would cooperate in supplying materials; that children would use light as a language, take pleasure in working alongside a friend, collaborate in a huge endeavor, and understand they were making something beautiful and permanent for their environment. The context was an experience in which project, materials, and documentation were inseparable. The connection to writing was the logical necessity for sequencing and manual dexterity.

Using Materials Fully

At an MELC Day in June 1995 Jennifer explained how she began to use materials:

> In parent conferences at the beginning of the year we asked what
> materials children had at home . . . scissors, crayons, glue. In
> reading the children's behavior and [in] conversations [with them],
> we saw that they must not have had experience with any materials
> like those in the Studio. Three-year-olds especially use the Studio
> to learn about paint, clay, plaster, colored water, the light table,
> cutting, gluing. Once children have some kind of base, we can
> make things. The Magic List helps me see how many times each
> child has engaged in an activity.

Jennifer's Magic List was a notebook with a page for each activity, children's names and symbols down the side. When a child used a particular material, Jennifer wrote the date next to the child's name. If there were few marks it indicated who had not used particular materials and which materials were underused.

Jennifer said:

> Materials have two lives. First, children explore materials' properties. For example, a teacher says, "Warren really needs help with cutting." Later, children use materials as another language to express their ideas, for example, the Communication project about friends sharing messages. The teachers and I read the conversations [their transcriptions of children's talk about sending messages], and decided to ask the children to draw their ideas. One by one, I brought children into the Studio: "You and Wendy had a conversation the other day. This is what you said. Would you like to draw it?" I shared the drawings with the other teachers who then gave me their notes so I knew what happened next.

> Everything we do is based on sharing information about everything that goes on. It's like a big circle of child to teacher; teacher to teacher, parent, and child; child to parent, and so on, linking children, teachers, families, ideas, feelings, and skills. Materials spur projects, which in turn are the subject of documentation.

ANATOMY OF A PROJECT

Projects have antecedents. They are always connected to prior activity and can lead to other things. The projects described below had rich themes and a long history in other experiences as the *9-1-1* project demonstrates.

Antecedents

The *9-1-1* project involved constructing a large ambulance from a cardboard box. It built on the children's interest in hospitals. The project began on April 29, 1994, but the first antecedents were in the fall of 1993. The annual mandatory health screening at D.C. General Hospital, which took place in October, frightened parents and children, so teachers organized get-acquainted field trips to the hospital. There the children saw ambulances coming and going. Panels about these trips fascinated parents and children all year, as did panels about Coco's trip to the animal hospital.

The *9-1-1* project had other antecedents. All year children had expanded their knowledge of materials—requesting, collecting, sorting, storing, exploring, and manipulating them. One material was boxes. On September 26, children made box constructions; on October 31, cut shapes to glue in boxes; on November 4, made box sculptures; on November 7, cut up boxes; on November 8, built with the cut-up pieces; on November 15, made box collages; and so on. The children often examined their box constructions and "read" the panels about them. Another antecedent was the teacher's March 30 survey on TV viewing in which the children indicated that *9-1-1* was a favorite TV program.

Connections

How did interest in hospitals, reading panels, box constructions, and a favorite TV program coalesce? From analyzing children's conversations and their responses to the survey, teachers noted that five children were particularly interested in the *9-1-1* program. On April 29, Wendy's questions—"What do you know about *9-1-1*?" and "What else do you want to know?"—triggered a long discussion. On May 3, Wendy read the children's answers back to them, then asked what they wanted to do next. Alonzo (5-3) responded immediately, "Draw an ambulance!" Another disussion, about ambulances' appearance, produced rich detail—front doors, rear doors, front lights, top emergency light, windows, wheels, stretcher, people, red cross, red stripe—and rich drawings.

On May 4, Jennifer engaged the children in a conversation about their ambulance drawings, and asked whether they preferred to turn their drawings into an ambulance made from clay or from a cardboard box. All chose a box, selecting the largest, about 2½' high by 4' long. The vehicle that emerged reflected the children's knowledge of ambulances from firsthand experience and TV, their use of boxes, and their familiarity with scissors, spray paint, glues, tape, nuts, bolts, and knives. Its complicated construction both consolidated and stretched their abilities (see Figure 9.2).

Another factor influencing the *9-1-1* project was the children's powers of observation. Constantly, in school and away, teachers urged them to observe carefully—classroom, weather, trees, people, streets, everything. Their observation skills were evident in the ambulance's many details. The antecedents had extended from fall to spring, involved different children and many media. As with any good project, *9-1-1* piqued imagination, sparked curiosity, demanded a big effort, required collaboration among teachers and children, and elicited joy. It also depended on an amalgam of experiences with different materials, and was compelled by the many panels that children "read" regularly.

DOCUMENTATION

Documentation is integral to projects. Children have hundreds of ideas—a pivotal question, a flash of intuition, a poetic expression—but they are often fleeting. One moment a child may be consumed by a caterpillar, the next by something entirely different, the momentary passion abandoned. If teachers can catch children's ideas on tape or preserve crucial moments in photos, if the child leaves a trace in a drawing or statement and teachers can represent it on a panel, it gives the moment permanence, enabling the child to continue the thought process.

Once Amelia asked the staff to stop working with children and work on documentation. She insisted they couldn't continue until the children considered what they'd done. The teachers resisted: "Ann doesn't want us to do this. We are teachers, employed to stay with the children." Amelia helped them rethink their

FIGURE 9.2. Thirteen figures surround the ambulance and a body on the stretcher. (Project *9-1-1*)

role, realize how essential self-reflection is in a child's development, and see documentation as the key to reflection.

9-1-1 Panels

Remaining all year, the ambulance, its documentation, and antecedent panels aroused interest, providing a context for many other experiences. First, the children who had constructed the ambulance showed it to the class; then they led tours of the panel, showing everyone, one small group at a time, how they made the ambulance. They "read" the panel to their classmates. They also pulled their families: "Come see what I've done!" Children didn't mention just one thing, but explained the entire experience. Their retelling stimulated conversation, aroused friends' interest, built families' confidence in the school, and highlighted the children's increasing articulateness. Visiting the documentation so excited the children, they decided to stage a puppet show about *9-1-1*.

Revisiting Panels

Over time, a process for revisiting panels developed. A teacher took the children who had worked on a project to "tour" its panel and recorded their comments. Together teachers reviewed the comments to determine if they'd missed something critical in constructing the panel. Revisiting panels became more formal:

The teacher who guided the tour took notes on the children's reactions, whether they paid attention, what they said, what they noticed.

Then, as a group, the teachers read the notes, eager for the feedback to see if the story made sense. Since only five children had made the ambulance, Wendy both guided the tour of the panel and took notes (if more than six, she would have taped). Wendy emphasized: "Even if it requires 2 hours, it's important to understand every word in a set of notes or a transcription; you never know what might trigger a connection to another teacher's observations or spur the children on."

Planning Panels

The commitment to make a panel was a "big deal" that would involve considerable work beyond the panel's construction. In planning meetings before starting a panel, teachers vigorously debated whether an activity needed to be documented. If so, how? with recorder? still camera? video? notes? sketch? Should they document the process? the entire experience? or one particular aspect?

With the *9-1-1* panel, they read Wendy's transcriptions about the *9-1-1* TV show and compared them to one another's notes or transcriptions from any part of the project. This material became the basis for the title, which they wrote first. Sometimes they wrote titles themselves, sometimes with children. Their notes were also the basis for a short paragraph, like a topic sentence, which they wrote together to explain the project's context and purpose. Because this paragraph was critical to understanding the story, they edited until they were sure it made sense. Finally they laid out the panel. The process enabled them to see if they needed other information: more research? a field trip? a visit to the hospital or library? Who would do it? Who would photograph? Amelia suggested questioning before the fact by considering how you would explain the experience to someone who wasn't there. To anticipate the next steps of a project, they read panels in progress. To see what they'd missed, they read the finished panel, relying on information gleaned from tours with the children to correct the story or augment the information. The process captured the essence of an experience and enabled them to better analyze what projects might happen next.

On an MELC Day (February, 1995) Jennifer remembered:

> [Our] first panel was on trains. We thought it was beautiful. Ann tried to read it, but always asked: "What is the story line? Why did you document this experience?" There was neither story nor motive. When Amelia asked the same questions, we were defensive. One day, Ann looked at the Trains panel and it had changed! She could understand because now it told a story!

The enormous effort the teachers had put into the first Trains panel was evident, so their defensiveness was understandable. Little was added to the revised panel. It contained far fewer words, but the changes focused the experience: The title, now a question and huge, grabbed attention, reflected the theme, and excited curiosity. The subtitle, also large, contained the answer in children's words. A new fifth photo sited the experience by showing them leaving on a field trip. Text and photos on the first panel wandered with no logical reason for the sequence or placement of text and images. The layout of the second panel was crisp, all thoughts sequential, all margins aligned. It was a big lesson for the teachers on how to create effective documentation.

Techniques

It is not obvious what to include, what information photographs should convey, or how to lay out a panel. When well done, a reader attends to the story, not the layout. But if something technical is amiss, it distracts a reader, the way it would if a book's type size deviated from page to page. A visitor commented: "It seems as if the school has a stenographer!" In fact, this was one of the teachers' roles, their notes a cross between an anthropologist's field record and their own subjective impressions.

Initially, teachers took photos of everything and made panels to fit. Instead, Amelia showed them how to use heavyweight white illustration board (30" × 40" Crescent X) and fit the material to it, standardizing the size. They developed a book with possible panel layouts for reference. In Reggio, documentation evolved to follow certain principles: white background, black type, standard overall size, font, placement of images; no extraneous decoration; children's work selected thoughtfully to illustrate main points; teacher notes including quick sketches to make the context clear. Panels were precisely designed and masterfully edited, skills in the *atelierista*'s repertoire that the other teachers learned too.

When Amelia presented gifts made by children at La Villetta, she directed the photo taking as a filmmaker would: "Get behind! Stand on a chair! Show the child's perspective, the backs of their heads, what they're looking at." They also photographed from across the circle to see gifts, faces, and body language in a single image. Teachers had to be in the experience and reflective about it simultaneously.

Jennifer explained what the teachers looked for in photos:

> We had lovely photos, but no context! Beautiful children were working on nice things, but the photos were superficial because they didn't show a stimulus or a process. We had to learn that photos, like photojournalism, must capture the moment an idea crystallizes and show how it evolves.

The teachers learned a process for constructing panels with *pre*thinking and *re*thinking as integral steps. As Amelia said, a panel is a kind of product with "a deep underlying structure in the stories" (MELC Day, February, 1995).

SOLVING PROBLEMS THROUGH PROJECTS

The following descriptions show teachers and children grappling with particular problems. Each shows how materials, projects, and documentation are interdependent, like three legs of a stool.

Problem: Deciding on a Subject for a Project

When teachers noticed, through their observations, notes, or recordings, that children were interested in something, they paid particular attention: That *something* could become the theme for a project. With a potential theme in mind, they listened to the tapes and read their notes to determine if the theme were rich enough and the children's interests strong enough to warrant following up. One such theme was photography. There had been a huge emphasis on photographs—requesting them from home, using them for the Families project and panel, adding photos throughout the environment. The teachers decided there *was* enough interest, that photography *would* be a strong theme. Having made that decision, they next brainstormed all the directions the project might take. Drawing on their recordings of children's conversations and daily notes, their brainstorming yielded this list: darkroom, negatives, film, slides, camera, light, subjects, enlargements, prints, costumes, chemicals, props, shadows, where to get film, tripods, developing, video camera, mirrors, exhibition.

Because of intense, simultaneous activity with letters, Sonya and the group interested in photographs had the idea of photographing objects in the environment—at school or outside—that resembled letters. Sonya took the children to purchase film, showed them how to use a camera, select the subject of a photograph, develop black-and-white film, and choose finished photographs for an exhibit. The project was called *Alphotography*. Its panel, with photographs by the children as well as photographs of them engaged in the activity, was mounted in the Library of the Big Room. The project revealed the process for selecting a project's theme, and demonstrated that children could recognize letters in unusual contexts.

Problem: Understanding a Child's Intent

The project Donald's Figures illustrates teachers' learning to question a child about his work. Donald (4-1), having used clay just once, made three figures; his excitement and pleasure were evident as he exclaimed: "Look, Jennifer!" Later, Amelia asked Donald to represent his figures in a different medium by drawing them in pencil. He did, and named each one.

The teachers noticed that two figures in the drawing were upside down. A long discussion ensued. Why had this happened? Should they ask Donald? Initially, they decided to ask questions indirectly so their ideas wouldn't overpower his. What should they say? Finally, Amelia simply asked, "Why?" "Because I like it!" Donald replied.

Jennifer tried a simple request: "Donald, tell me about your picture." Donald, adding to his drawing with no comment about the upside-down-ness, responded, "I forgot the stomach."

Stymied, the teachers conferred again, and decided to ask directly why the figures were upside down. "Oh," said Donald, matter-of-factly lifting two corners of the paper until two figures stood upright, "they're talking to each other."

What had stymied the teachers was of no consequence to the child. Why should it be? He envisioned the figures standing and facing each other, an entirely different relation than the teachers saw. Their sense of spatial orientation in two dimensions simply did not match Donald's. The project showed Donald's competence in visualizing a figure from a multitude of perspectives, and how little teachers may know about what a child is thinking.

Problem: Determining Proportion, Managing Scope

The project Alonzo's Dinosaur shows teacher and child translating from one medium to another, sculpture to drawing, and how they collaborated on two big problems—changing scale and the project's enormity. To give the museum presence in the school, Jennifer borrowed some sculpture by Nek Chand, a folk artist from Chandighar, India. She stood the largest piece, a creature about 3½' high by 5' long, in front of the Studio's mirrors. The creature had a double beak made from spouts of two green glass bottles. It was formed over bent rebar, and shaped with cement in which irregular pieces of broken green glass were embedded, covering the entire figure so that it glistened. The children were extremely excited to discover it and called it a dinosaur, although it was really more birdlike. Alonzo wanted to make one. The teachers concluded it was an opportunity to explore transferring from a three- to a two-dimensional medium.

The project was provoked by the teachers' adding a collection of small plastic dinosaurs to the block area, then observing to see who was most interested. When they considered who was most likely to remain interested, they chose Alonzo, knowing he loved dinosaurs, but had a problem drawing.

On November 29 Jennifer brought three children who loved drawing and Alonzo, who had hardly drawn at all, to the Studio. Together they explored the sculpture, touching and talking about it. Then Jennifer presented four large sheets of paper, pencils, and Unibal pens, whose fine points capture great detail. They talked about the materials, the differences between pens and pencils, that pencil lines can be lightened and erased. And the children drew.

The next day, after examining their drawings, Jennifer invited Alonzo, whose drawing looked most like the sculpture, to the Studio. Through her careful documentation—in notes and photos—we see teacher and child struggling with the immense challenge of scaling a large sculpture on paper. She asked if Alonzo wanted to make a second drawing more closely resembling the sculpture. He was discouraged; his first drawing had a short, stubby tail—a longer one wouldn't fit on the paper! Jennifer considered this her first mistake: She had not provided paper in correct proportion. The sculpture was rectangular and long, but she had furnished squarish paper.

Jennifer noted: "Realizing that he did not have space to add feet, Alonzo began again, adding a second drawing above the first, but there still wasn't room for feet." She gave him more paper and he drew a third. This time his shape was better, but the proportion of the paper was still not correct, and again there was no room for feet. Jennifer considered this her mistake too; again she'd given him out-of-proportion paper.

The next day Jennifer gave Alonzo a huge piece of paper, the size of the whole table, and said, "I see three drawings. Which is the real one?" Together they studied the problem. When Alonzo indicated which drawing he liked, she commented,

"I don't see any legs." Years later Jennifer said, "How could I say that? Terrible comment! First-year teacher! I should have engaged him in a dialogue to analyze the problem."

Alonzo suggested cutting out the dinosaur and putting it on a new piece of paper since this paper already had three dinosaurs and definitely no room for feet! So Jennifer cut it out, they glued it on a new sheet, and Jennifer taped on more paper. This time the feet were accurate but the beak did not resemble the sculpture. Realizing she had been too directive, Jennifer now said, "I don't know what to do." Alonzo left the drawing, walked across the room, and examined the sculpture. Then he asked Jennifer to add more paper, and redrew the beak. But he was not pleased; there were erasures, taped-on papers, and mistakes.

On the third day Alonzo drew a final version on new paper. Then he tried the tail. First he made a square, but the tail looked like a flag. He couldn't figure out the proportion, and kept walking back and forth examining the sculpture. He even rested his finger on the paper and drew its outline. Finally, he produced a drawing that pleased him. Feet, beak, tail—and all were correctly proportioned. It took him 2 more days to draw all the odd shapes representing the pieces of glass— a huge undertaking, or "Sweaty," in Alonzo's word. The drawing was enormous, about as large as the sculpture, detailed, and amazingly accurate.

But another big problem occurred: how to add color. Alonzo did not want to use crayons or watercolor; it would be too much work to fill all the shapes. Jennifer, Amelia, and Alonzo conferred—a long discussion—sharing ideas, negotiating, brainstorming. Finally, a plan emerged: They would trace the outline on a new piece of paper, paint it with large brushes using green watercolor, then carefully cut Alonzo's shapes and glue them onto the painted background. This would take the least effort. Because he had drawn the shapes on translucent paper and the glue was clear, the painted background would show through.

All three put his drawing on the floor and together traced the perimeter and the hundred or so interior shapes. While Alonzo mixed paint and watercolored the new background, the teachers cut out the interior shapes with X-Acto knives. Then Alonzo glued the shapes onto the newly painted background while Jennifer prepared the documentation: Alonzo's finished piece, small-scale drawings (Jennifer's copies) of interim stages, Alonzo's statements, and Jennifer's written interpretation of the entire process.

Eight days after his first drawing, Alonzo finished. He was so proud! He brought his entire family including grandmother, cousins, and aunt. His classmates insisted visitors see it the minute they arrived. He left for first grade next fall, his dinosaur still hanging. His mother came often, so happy to see his dinosaur still displayed. The project showed that a very young child will stick to an enormously challenging project. Jennifer said the project was a big learning process for her. The project prepared Alonzo to recognize shapes and distinguish their orientation, essential skills in learning to identify letters.

Problem: Integrating Project and Panel

The Pollution project, which Wendy did with seven children, began on September 29, 1993, with a visit to the White House. Four children attended a press conference held by the Clinton administration: Detroit CEOs were agreeing to collaborate on research about clean cars. The children's drawings of cars were on display. The children reported back on the visit at a full-group meeting. Later, the teachers made a panel about the experience, triggering many discussions: What did the press conference mean? How do cars pollute? How can future cars be clean? How can people make life better? At all stages, the children described their ideas in words and drawings that the teachers recorded in photos, in notes, and on tape, and turned into panels.

The teachers asked the most interested children for ideas about what causes pollution. They did field research—watching passing cars, visiting a gas station, trying to determine where pollution comes from, whether it's in the gas. Each child had a theory, which the teachers displayed on a panel. Renée's theory, "Pollution is everywhere, on houses, cars, and in water," connected pollution with cars. The number of panels on pollution was increasing, revisited and "read" often by the children.

Early in December a health alert occurred: Washington water was unsafe to drink. The children brought bottled water to school along with many questions and the knowledge that the water was dangerous, dirty, and could make them sick. They were very upset, wanting to know why it had happened. Eric said, "It made me angry!" More impassioned conversations and lively drawings ensued about what pollution is and where it comes from. The children knew a TV program in which the character Pollution tries to kill Captain Planet.

In February, with the topic still generating interest, the children decided to pollute some water. Wendy and Jennifer considered what might happen, and listed photos they might need, such as collecting materials, dirtying water, researching. This helped them determine who would take the photos and when. First, the children filled a basin with water. They added dirt from flower pots, then brown paint, then clay. Their first idea to purify the water was to add soap. Photos showed their consternation when dishwashing detergent made the water foam but did not clean it, even when they stirred it vigorously. They decided to sleep on the problem. The next day they added hand lotion. More mess! More consternation! Another night's sleep. Neither soap powder nor ice worked. They put the mixture in the sun—nothing worked. They decided to consult the dictionary, but found no suggestions there.

Many lengthy discussions ensued. Then there was a breakthrough, described by Galeesa: "Renée figured out that we could go to the library and we did, . . . and then we look in the books!" The group made several trips to search for a solution, pouring over dozens of books on water and pollution. On March 8 they found a book that described how to clean dirty water. Teachers' photos captured the children's excitement as they discovered a page with a diagram of a water-filtering system.

At full-group meeting on March 9, Wendy asked Renée and DeMarcos to report on where they'd gone yesterday. As the discussion ensued, she asked, "Why don't we all revisit the water experiment panel?" Spread across six panels were the White House visit, drawings of future cars, theories about pollution, making dirty water, and attempts to make clean water. The children recounted how, yesterday, at the library they had found just what they needed in a reference book, and copied the page. They were so excited, they decided to draw filtering systems. The trip and their drawings became the subject for another panel.

Next morning at full-group meeting Jennifer asked, "Can we look at what you brought back?" The five showed the class the page. Instructions included a diagram of the system and a list of what they needed to make one: dirty water (which the teachers had saved in jars), sand, gravel, cotton, pebbles, a cup, and a large plastic bottle. The five decided to make a filtering system immediately! Searching the school, within an hour they'd found everything on the list, built the system, and by 11:00 were adding the filtering materials (see Figure 9.3). Finally, the culmination: They poured in the dirty water, added clean water to flush it through, and watched. Bubbles came up. But, nothing else happened.

Wendy asked, "Do you think we have to wait for all this water to go down?" They decided to have lunch. Afterward, they raced back to the Studio. DeMarcos arrived first and screamed, "Hey, y'all, it work!" Renée, amazed, "It's clean!" Galeesa, astonished, "It's not dark anymore." Anthony beamed, "Clean water!" The result so delighted the children that Jennifer reiterated the caution on the reference page: "Do *not* drink the filtered water. It may not be clean enough."

Together teachers and children created a display near the pollution panels. It included the reference page, reduced reproductions of their diagrams, the filtering system itself, the dirty and cleaned water, related books, and a panel about the experience. Everyone revisited the area often, especially as Washington's water problems continued, using the documentation to "read" the stories to themselves and visitors, later deciding to visit the city's water treatment center to learn how water becomes clean enough to drink. The project showed how young children's

FIGURE 9.3. The group added filtering materials to the system. (Studio)

concern about the environment can be nurtured and become a springboard for the kind of science project generally undertaken by much older children.

IT WAS A VERY FINE YEAR

Even early in fall 1993, Sonya and Wendy realized the importance of documentation:

> Today as the children came out of the Nap Room, they noticed a new panel. . . . Usually a sleepy trying-to-wake-up time, . . . this afternoon [they] immediately became alive in conversation, sharing stories, pointing to pictures, and discussing what they remembered. We watched smiling . . . [observing] how positively the children are responding to this kind of provocation. (Memo, October 27, 1993)

Wendy realized, "Panels help parents understand the true intellectual nature of a child's mind, questioning, and following ideas with materials." Jennifer added, "I have a much clearer idea now about the purposes of panels, how effective they are for parents and for teachers to review projects and see new ideas in photos. They have a dual advantage, for the teacher as much as the child" (MELC Day, November 1994).

The Capitol project proved they could sustain a project from one school year to another, weaving different children in and out. Other projects showed them what complex things the children could do and how involved their families could become. All the projects showed the teachers' growth in scaffolding children's interests—supporting them with their own astute observation, their own multiple perspectives as teachers, wide-ranging materials, and use of various environments in and out of school. On an MELC Day Wendy said, "The teachers don't know how something is going to turn out, how limitless a hypothesis can be, like an octopus" (September 1994). Sonya noted how important panels were to parents: "Parents made observations about the changes they noticed [in photos on the panels] in their children from the beginning to now" (Memo, March 24, 1994). Wendy was thrilled when parents sent materials from home that related to the panels. Whitney's mother said, "Where there was home researches [*sic*], the whole family participated. . . . It seemed the family liked the project even more than Whitney did" (Lewin, 1998, p. 356). Teachers observed other educators intently studying the panels, awed by what they revealed, curious about how projects happened, looking for a connection between what they saw here and their own teaching, awakened to the relationship between rich experiences and literacy.

CHAPTER 10

Our Families,
Other Educators

It is not new to include thinking, problem solving, and reasoning in someone's *school curriculum, it is new to include it in* everyone's. . . . *We must view this . . . as an invitation to inventive and very demanding educational reform.*

Lauren Resnick

If you'd asked the teachers at the beginning of school year 1992–93 whether they could meet the challenges of becoming collaborators in the spirit of Reggio teachers, they might have hesitated. Had they understood exactly what that entailed, they would have demurred. But each achievement, even the first tentative ones, provided a strong incentive to continue. By spring 1994 they realized that their colleagues' negative comments were not pejorative barbs but sincere help; that your insecurities, if openly discussed with a supportive group, could improve your performance. They were beginning to bare their souls to one another, to abandon solo performance for reciprocal process, and to replace competitive motives with collaborative spirit. They were adopting a teaching style characterized by the rigor and intensity of the best artists and scientists.

In brief, they learned to trust one another. Trust is based on mutual respect and builds over time, deepening when people speak truthfully. Thoreau said, "We may safely trust a good deal more than we do. We may waive . . . [as] much care of ourselves as we honestly bestow elsewhere" (1854/1965, p. 6). Few people find anyone to whom to waive care, least of all at work. Learning to trust changed the teachers' relationships to one another and now they expected trust in all their work relationships. They were prime examples of a mission-driven staff, focused exclusively on the classroom, committed to intense demands:

> The project is all they see. . . . [They] are . . . indefatigable people . . . struggling to turn a vision into a machine and whose lawns and goldfish have died of neglect. . . . [They] have only one passion—the task at hand. . . . [They] don't want to talk about anything else, be anywhere else, do anything else. (Bennis & Biederman, 1997, p. 208)

Above all, they learned that the greatest joy is participating as young children's intelligence grows, that nothing is more invigorating than children's energy when it is focused on challenges that capture their total being. As facilitator, not collaborator, I eagerly followed each project, examined each new panel, and praised every accomplishment, struck by the dramatic growth reflecting the teachers' changed relationships.

If one year seems short for such momentous change, consider what is typical. New math, introduced in the 1970s, was based on sound ideas of how children learn and full of engaging lessons illustrating important math concepts. Ultimately it failed. It necessitated unfamiliar teaching techniques: one-on-one instruction, small-group activity, use of manipulative materials, reorganization of space. But few teachers are educated to work this way. Moreover, if children have not been taught to act independently, they won't use time well on their own, which children must do when a teacher uses individual or small-group instruction.

Mostly, teachers were expected to use new math with 2 days' training, for some perhaps 2 weeks. The few specialists were responsible for far more schools than could be served. Unfortunately, many curricular changes are introduced in such circumstances—inadequate help for teachers, no match between beliefs already in place and those undergirding the new approach, few classroom structures to support change. Compared to doctors' or lawyers' training, the teachers' 9 months with Amelia seem short. But, compared to the time teachers usually are given, it was enormous.

In this chapter, I describe the growth in the family program and reveal how MELC Days heightened the teachers' awareness of their craft. I also recount the teachers' own reflections at year-end, during an examination for accreditation by Reggio Children, on how they had changed.

INVOLVING FAMILIES

In Reggio, family involvement is as important as everything else. Malaguzzi told our March 1992 delegation:

> Families have a great hunger for information, even when you hardly
> ever see them. It is impossible in a society where information has
> such huge value for the *school* not to give information as well—we
> need antennae on the roof to constantly transmit information. The
> exchange of information becomes an exchange of values and ideas.
> This is why we think of child, adult, and family all together.

Amelia showed us how to look at everything—environment, celebrations, outings, organization—both from the family's perspective and as a means to involve them.

Changing a Mind-Set

The first step was to establish a role for the families. But, how? In many meetings Amelia helped us examine our ideas about our families. We talked about whether each child lived in a nuclear or extended family, or lived with friends. We pooled our evidence of specific conditions in each child's life, and anecdotes about particular episodes, like children coming to school hungry or meeting one of our families outside the school and displaying physical signs that either a child or a mother had been abused. We reexamined the children's conversations and con-nected their references to guns, drugs, police, moms in jail, fighting, and violence to specific children. The personal profiles revealed the enormity of our families' problems. The question was what our points of intersection with these families could be.

The issues were huge. In endless hours of discussion (and I cannot overem-phasize *hours* and *discussion*), a direction slowly emerged: to focus on finding a small number of very specific ways to encourage families to participate. In more long discussions we determined we would communicate, socialize, and exchange spe-cific information. But, how? At length, we decided on an initial step: Delineate a wide range of possibilities for family participation. We wanted to create many opportunities to make them integral to everything that went on, to highlight the importance of their presence in the school, and, simultaneously, motivate them to *be* a presence, for their sake and their children's. Amelia explained that families, as well as children, should be protagonists for projects.

The challenges were to help families realize the importance of what took place in school and to improve the quality of our daily relationships with them. But, the teachers worried, to what extent could we ask families to contribute to the school? Believing the families had little to contribute, the teachers were uneasy about asking for *anything*. They saw families' circumstances and lack of financial resources as impenetrable barriers and were afraid of intruding. Amelia taught us to dissolve the barriers, to understand that poverty does not stop life. People are people re-gardless, and family life, by its very nature, is rich. Any family is a wealth of rela-tionships, life experiences, and values.

Welcoming Families In

We started by making the child visible, not just children as biological off-spring, but as people with rights, and childhood as a human condition. Simulta-neously, we made all our activities visible—the impetus behind the fall 1993 effort to mount so much documentation. And it *was* an effort: Do, Document, Mount, again and again between October and Thanksgiving, filling wall after wall with panels.

Because of the Greeting Room's importance, it was the first place we changed. By June 1994, that small space overflowed with information. There, like in a table of contents, parents could see at a glance their children, the nature of the school, the reasons for its existence, what went on, the people who were part of it, the com-munities of which it was part, and above all where they fit in.

When we visited Reggio Emilia in March 1992, Malaguzzi said, "It is im-portant for the school to demonstrate to the parents and to the family the theoreti-cal nucleus of the program, that the children are rich, strong, and powerful." The Outer and Inner Greeting Rooms did that. The former contained the mission state-ment (see Chapter 3), information about the MELC-Museum-Washington relation-ship, about the MELC-Reggio link, and news clips about Reggio schools and the MELC.

Immediately inside the Inner Greeting Room were two panels; one provided a succinct overview of the school—hours, number of children, flow of the day, with children's drawings and photos of them at various activities. The second panel was titled Some Examples of Messages for Parents and showed families what they would find on the Parent Board. It had a copy of the letter home about new birthday party procedures and a notice, "The Dining Room Needs Your Help"; both panels had children's words and drawings. The Parent Board, as large as a panel, had other information, most done with children's involvement—copies of current messages home, weekly and monthly schedules, upcoming events, requests for materials or help, announcements, news clips. It became common for family members to stand at the Parent Board reviewing the schedules (see Figure 10.1), then to look at photos of themselves doing so. The photos emphasized that messages were meant to be read. They amplified the messages' importance, giving them status, as media attention always does. Russell's mother said, "The parent board is especially helpful. It's a great way to communicate" (Lewin, 1998, p. 356). Jesse's mother commented, "I read the journal on the parent board every day. This is the best way for me to know what is going on" (p. 355). The Parent Board became a vital connection between school and home.

Monthly schedules contained certainties like birthdays, field trips, and issues raised in parent-teacher meetings. Descriptions of a school can be organized in many ways; the MELC's monthly schedule was organized solely from families' perspective. This one-page document had 8 headings which reflected every area involving the home-school connection: Staff Meetings, Meetings with Families, Projects with Families, Field Trips, Parties/Celebrations, Seminars/Workshops, Training, Social Services. The information started dialogues because the families asked questions about it.

FIGURE 10.1. A parent studies the Parent Board. (Greeting Room)

For children, the process was transparent: Teachers discussed every flyer, so they knew what their families would receive. Children took the messages home and heard them read there. Evidence of their children, through drawings or writing, immediately hooked the parents. Correspondence demonstrated that children, teachers, and families all had roles. During school year 1993–94, the teachers sent home over 66 pieces of correspondence. A copy of each was added to the records accumulating in the Greeting Room, well organized and readily accessible.

Connections with families were also strengthened through books the teachers made with past years' photos. Families particularly liked finding theirs. Books were kept on top of the shelves in the Inner Greeting Room where weekly and monthly summaries and messages accumulated, organized in separate folders. The combination of last year's books and this year's records told the full story of life at school, providing a record of the children's changes, showing their continuous history. They were similar to a piece of documentation Carlina called A Child's Autobiography as a Learner that records how children change, a record Reggio teachers consider 4-year-olds' birthright. Carlina compared it to someone unknown, centuries ago, inventing musical notation so we can remember familiar songs: "As notation shows how a tune changes, documentation shows how a child changes, and is the most powerful way to bind families to a school." Jesse's mother understood: "The documentation [let me] . . . know what was happening in the school over a span of time" (Lewin, 1998, p. 355).

In the Inner Greeting Room, Wendy welcomed children, the morning transition from home to school. Parents asked, "Miss Wendy, can I help so you can sit in the chair?" It was reassuring to see her there, receive her welcome, watch her embrace their child.

In addition to schedules, memos, and history, the staff personalized the entry with photographs of teachers, children, and families, setting the stage for dialogue. Family members saw these images first, and felt expected, desired. They began to realize, from both panels and the huge volume of communication, that they mattered, that the school was a place that valued them. When one considers how isolated many families are, it is sad to realize that these techniques, which cost so little and yet transform isolation to inclusion, are not widely used.

Seeing the School Through Panels

Another place families knew intimately was the Book Sharing Area. Daisica's grandmother said, "I thoroughly enjoyed the book sharing program . . . sending books home every day. Sometimes I read them, . . . sometimes her grandfather. . . . This routine . . . helped me to become part of the school and was valuable for Daisica's learning" (Lewin, 1998, p. 355). Beside the table hung a favorite panel— trips to the hospital. It arrested both children's and families' attention since hospitals, with their implied emergencies, are scary. Family members quizzed the teachers about the panel, their questions sharpening teachers' awareness of what is most important to photograph and document, more reciprocal learning.

Interest in the hospital panel provided an opening for teachers to explain how children toured the school with a teacher revisiting documentation. Whitney's mother said, "The panels helped me a lot in understanding the projects. . . . [I]t was so clear. The words and the pictures explain everything. One of the children will explain to you, and help you understand the panels, because they know what they have done" (Lewin, 1998, p. 356).

The first things teachers requested from home were photos for a panel, Our Families and Us. It made the connection between home and school real, and motivated other families to send photos. When needed, teachers sent the camera home, impetus for the Alphotography project. The Families panel became a month-and-a-half-long project, children augmenting family photos with their own words and drawings.

The staff had labored to complete and hang panels on all fall 1993 activities prior to the Thanksgiving Feast. In only 2 months, walls that were bare in September by comparison became covered with documentation, alive with images of family members, children, projects, celebrations, new systems. Unaware of the enormous effort, families were thoroughly engaged. Obvious favorites, because they contained family photos, were the Pumpkin Patch, Fall, and Families panels, covering long walls outside the Nap Room. Panels reflected such varied activities that the children became visible to the families. Daisica's grandmother said, "The panels . . . lit up the school. . . . I love it! It . . . helped to understand what was going on" (Lewin, 1998, p. 355).

Family Meetings

There were surprises at the first family meeting on October 6—fruit prepared by the children, a folder for each family with information about teachers and children, and copies of transcribed conversations so families could "hear" the school in their children's words. Karlisa's mother appreciated "how you put down the children's dialogues word for word as the children said them" (Lewin, 1998, p. 355).

In November, the teachers became concerned about the commercialism and burdens that too often accompany the holidays, and raised the issue in a letter home on December 2. A lengthy discussion ensued at the December 8 parent meeting about values. Some families wanted *no* involvement with Christmas. It was decided that children and families would make presents for one another and for the school. The Parent-Teacher Committee would arrange details.

Shortly thereafter, the Committee decided to use the Parent Room for families to wrap gifts for their children. Toward Christmas teachers stocked the room with wrapping materials, pencils, and a pad for each child. Committee members wrapped the gifts for families who could not come to school. As the holiday approached, some family members worked with Jennifer after school in the Studio to make light boxes, their gifts to the school. As a surprise, the teachers made each family a book with frequently sung songs illustrated by the children. There was no Santa Claus because everyone had agreed to emphasize holidays as times for families to be together and share.

Seventeen family meetings were held in 1993–94, in addition to field trips, outings, birthday celebrations, other special occasions, and meetings of the Parent-Teacher Committee. Reginold's mother said, "Every day I can see the panels, but sometimes I can't get a chance to read the walls. The meetings really helped me to know what to look at, and what to pay attention to. I've never been bored. The meetings were always very interesting" (Lewin, 1998, p. 354). Russell's mother agreed, "Parent meetings were most helpful for me. All of them. . . . They let me know what is going on" (p. 356).

In school year 1993–94 there were 40 different formally organized occasions for families. Each was attended by, on average, 30 families: individual fall meetings with every family; spring meetings with families of children leaving; work sessions to plan meetings or events. The Parent-Teacher Committee had its own meetings arranging fund-raising events, parties, festivals. Reginold's mother said:

> Parent meetings were what helped me the most. Real wonderful meetings! I appreciated that you talked in detail about the children. The meetings were not based on [making] decisions, but on what the children were doing. Because I know what the children were doing, I felt I could go ahead and know what *I* should do. (Lewin, 1998, p. 354)

Whitney's mother said, "I liked the big parent meetings because it was good to hear what the other parents had to say, and this was a good way for everyone to voice their opinions." She joked, "Sometimes the eating part got out of hand!" (pp. 355, 356).

Birthday Celebrations

Birthday celebrations were a favorite activity, but painful for children whose party never materialized. Moreover, families felt competitive because refreshments and gifts from home varied greatly. So the Parent-Teacher Committee developed new procedures. On October 17, the teachers wrote, and the children illustrated, a letter explaining that the new procedures would help all children feel valued and build friendships in meaningful ways.

Jennifer made a Birthday Calendar and panel that became extremely popular. They covered a large wall in the Dining Room where celebrations were held. Empty at first, they were provocations: Find *your* photo; look for the date of *your* birthday. Whitney's mother liked the fact they had all the children's names and birthdays. Birthdays became *big* events.

Teachers held conversations with a small group of the birthday child's closest friends about presents, birthday card, cake, where the party would take place, flowers, decorations. Presents required intense deliberation and extensive work in the Studio, closest friends making them in secret. There was lots of suspense. Truly wondrous gifts emerged. Children broke into huge smiles as they unwrapped their gifts. One received an elaborate book of her closest friends' portraits. Another received a huge car, a truly incredible construction his friends created. Galeesa exclaimed, "That's his car! A big car! It was beautiful!" On Aisha's birthday, Lorian crowed, "And she got a card too. The card had stars on it. She was so happy." It was an emotional time, children hugging each other appreciatively, gifts reflecting their deep knowledge of one another.

Communication

Karlisa's mother said, "I couldn't . . . be as active as I would have liked. I relied on the messages for my information—my understanding of the school and the teachers" (Lewin, 1998, p. 355). With so much emphasis on messages, the teachers introduced families to the Communication Center with its well-stocked work counter, word processing software, and mailboxes. They focused on the question, What is a message?, explaining that children were communicating with one another and with children at Amelia's school in Italy.

The strong interest in messages led to a Post Office project, children actually following a letter on its journey. A father who was a mailman came to school, in uniform with mail sack, for children to interview. Families particularly enjoyed this project because it featured a parent in the documentation. It began a new area of involvement—making children familiar with family members' work.

It is important for families to help the school change. But, Amelia cautioned, you cannot ask for help without explaining why things are being changed, why you are asking. The more communication the school provides, the more the families know, the better children fare, and the more the families become involved. Renée's mother said, "As for having input into the school, I input a whole lot, you know that" (Lewin, 1998, p. 355).

Respecting Children's Speech

During discussions on literacy, Karlisa's mother expressed her anger. Waving a transcription for all to see, she declared emphatically:

> I'm going to bring this to Karlisa's school [next year] and show them how you *listened* to my child and wrote down *exactly* what she said. I don't think it's right to consider *proper* English as what must be spoken or taught all the time. As long as they get the point across, who cares? Maybe it's because *you* [teachers] can't understand *them* [children], not because they can't communicate. You want to change the way I hear this at home? I resent that. Let the children speak their language. I'm going to read *this* [to next year's teachers]. (Lewin, 1998, p. 355)

Her point, that if children are to speak at all they first must be listened to, was valid. The verbatim transcriptions gave families evidence that the MELC teachers did listen. Transcripts and children's quotes on panels proved that the teachers respected what children had to say, which in turn built families' trust.

Parent-Teacher Committee

The Parent-Teacher Committee was reorganized in 1993–94, spurred by Amelia's expertise. A subcommittee of all family members, it had two teachers and those five family members with the interest and time. It was responsible for communication and liaison between the teachers and all the families. Between October and May it met six times, brought order to the parent program, gave family members who so desired more involvement, and provided an effective network among families. It relieved the teachers, vastly improving prior years when parents vied competitively for titles like president and vice president in an organization with no defined functions.

The highlight for families in fall 1993 was the trip the committee organized to the pumpkin patch, attended by 32 children, 13 parents, and 6 staff. Children went on a hay ride, and each family selected a pumpkin. Domonique's mother said:

> I enjoyed the field trips most! I especially like the field trips to the arbore-tum. I feel these experiences opened up the children more, and encouraged them to talk more, and to ask more questions. A lot of parents came on the field trips, and so I got to know them better, and the other children too. Also, I got to bring my youngest son on the trips . . . a great opportunity for him. (Lewin, 1998 p. 355)

The committee also organized two other fall activities. There was an Octoberfest on the playground with the families' pumpkins and home-cooked food. With great ceremony teachers and parents removed the Fall panel, carried it to the playground, and rested it carefully against the fence. It was the focal point of the Fest, showcasing families' involvement in a panoply of experiences. There was also a Thanksgiving feast. Nineteen family members attended the prefeast slide show and 32 attended the feast itself, eating and socializing.

All year, discussions at staff meetings reflected the emphasis on families—29 long discussions about family involvement, 9 in October alone. By June families were deeply involved, comfortable working together, practiced at organizing di-verse efforts. It required only one meeting to plan the June 14 Graduation Day Ceremony and Cookout and the June 22 Big Summer Birthday Party for the five children with summer birthdays.

School and Families Connected

Gradually, as 1993–94 proceeded and we communicated what was happen-ing through letters, memos, field trips, panels, and the Parent Board, families be-came aware of the school, realized they could express their needs and desires, and understood they had rights. It happened in little ways: Reginold's father stood observing from the door to the Big Room. Later he told us how much he learned about discipline watching us handle the children. Derrick's family asked to bor-row the camera. Many parents brought extended family members to meetings or celebrations. Mrs. Dickerson volunteered to donate decorations for the holiday party. Rickie's grandmother said:

> I wasn't the family member who came most frequently; Rickie's aunt and great-grandmother came to most things. Rickie's great-grandmother . . . thoroughly enjoyed all of the events, and spoke of them often. I did come to the Octoberfest last year . . . [where] I had the chance to meet all the chil-dren Rickie talked about. . . . This is not a place where you just drop your child off. You can see what children are involved in, through the pictures around, and you can see children enjoying themselves in what they are doing. (Lewin, 1998, p. 355).

Families had become aware of ways they and the school could support one another. Renée's mother said:

> I must have asked about 500 questions. . . . I was new at the motherhood game, but I'm doing it. Whatever I asked, you all took care of it. . . . [Panels are] good.

> It reminds the children of what they've done, and it helps the parents too. They must help the visitors to see what you do. Maybe the D.C. Council members should come here and see them! (Lewin, 1998, pp. 355–356)

Perhaps she sensed that District officials should know more about us.

In November 1994 on an MELC Day, Amelia said, "Our parents—many living at the margins of 'mainstream society'—have found a place for themselves in the school and have been helped to construct a powerful image of their children" (Lewin, 1998, p. 352). By turning 44-hour weeks into 60, Amelia had shown us how to make families' presence evident everywhere: in panels, in the success of MELC Days, and especially in the robust parent program. Finally, the teachers understood what Amelia meant when she remarked, "Having no families involved in a school is like having a body without arms."

Recalling the beginning of school year 1993–94, when the course was so unclear, we could see that, in fact, we had succeeded in exploring values, sharing resources, and fostering exchanges between home and school. Amelia confirmed : "Families understand how important it is to us to support them, help them, consider them. Today, the school is perceived by families as a precious jewel, almost a redemption." (MELC Day, April, 1995).

VISITS FROM EDUCATORS

The success of the June 1993 Reggio Emilia Symposium, the brief visits by symposium participants to the MELC, and news articles about the MELC generated scores of requests for visits. They came from teams of teachers trying to rethink their own goals, educators who had heard of the Reggio Approach, and teacher educators. Soon after arriving in September 1993, Amelia proposed a formal program so other educators could learn about the MELC, but I disagreed, concerned that the teachers were overextended. Amelia persisted, arguing that we had a responsibility to show other educators what we were doing, and that it would be important for our teachers. We finally resolved that we would invite educators for a fee to a one-day program, A Day in the MELC (later called simply MELC Days), structured not to burden the teachers. The program ran 2 days in a row, each day for a different group of about 40. In the morning Amelia, two teachers, and I presented history and basic information, then visitors observed the children. After their lunch visitors toured the school independently while the children napped, then we answered their questions until 5.

Attendees came from all over. There was always more demand than we could accommodate. In school year 1993–94 the first MELC Day took place on October 6, 1993, the next in February 1994, the last in June. In school year 1994–95 MELC Days, again 2 days in succession for different groups, were held in September, November, February, April, and June (see Figure 10.2).

Visitors noticed the immense effort, the evidence of teachers' collaboration, mutual respect, and trust. They saw how the teachers needed one another, how each one's work was strengthened by the others. They observed the wealth of children's work, its visual richness and complexity. They saw the families everywhere on panels and noticed items from home throughout the school. They felt these

FIGURE 10.2. Planning an MELC Day (left to right): Ann, Genet, Jennifer, Wendy, and Sonya. (Studio)

results were unusual and asked many questions about how they could adapt the Reggio approach.

New Perspectives

Educators' questions sharpened the teachers' focus on the "why" of their practices. We recorded visitors' questions and studied them. Preparing for MELC Days and analyzing educators' responses deepened the teachers' appreciation for the Reggio Approach. Their performance came into high relief as they structured MELC Days and answered questions. Many questions related to classroom management. Some were about teacher renewal, others about panels. Most were about materials. The huge amount overwhelmed visitors; incredulous, they asked if the children really used everything. Yes! The children used it all. Because of the ultimate order, the conversations about each material's purpose, and their involvement in the lives of materials, children used them well.

Isn't the Capitol project too complex for the children? Oh, dear, this question could only be answered with questions: Why would you think so? Was it the subject matter? the length of time children were involved? or the activities? Did you see in the photos how engrossed the children were? Was their excitement as visible to you as to us? Did you recognize their enormous effort to express their reactions to an event they watched from their own windows? What is your image of young children? No, we did not find it too complex.

To us, the question reflected thinking shaped by lesson plans, and failure to grasp very young children's immense capacity to notice everything, to ponder difficult questions, to engage in complex activity. That mind-set does not recognize young children's urgency to be part of the world around them, to understand its events. The Capitol project began when a parent sent a newspaper clipping relating that the statue atop the dome of the U.S. Capitol building would soon be removed for cleaning. The article came from home and, valuing every home contact, we read it to the children. It instantly grabbed their attention because the dome dominated the view from so many of the MELC's windows. And we were off on a project in which the children re-created and the teachers documented every step in the months-long removal, cleaning, and reinstallation of the statue.

A Reflexive Process

On MELC Days we shared our experiences with strangers, our pain and joy. Their empathy made us value those experiences more. Their questions made us thoughtful. Their criticism strengthened our bonds to one another. There was more praise than criticism, and the adulation buoyed our spirits. The teachers perfected their performance: Initially motivated by their role as researchers, now they were also preparing for an audience.

That audience was hungry for new ideas, grateful for the opportunity to visit. Typical comments were: "Thank you for an inspirational day. I am anxious to return to my classroom of 3-year-olds to begin to assess how I can implement some of these ideas." Or, "Thank you for helping us remember why we chose this profession" (November, 1994). The teachers began to anticipate MELC Days eagerly.

MELC Days put a new focus on documentation: Revisiting panels to explain their experiences increased the teachers' understanding. After each MELC Day they reentered the classroom with others' questions in mind. These echoes heightened their awareness of the nuances of their practice, giving them new eyes with which to see connections between their beliefs, their words, and their actions.

A MODEL EARLY LEARNING CENTER

In June 1994 we had an unusual opportunity to hear reactions from educators whom we esteemed: Vea Vecchi and Carlina Rinaldi examined the MELC for accreditation by Reggio Children (granted in September 1994). These two educators, ultimate master teachers, observed the school, took note of everything, then questioned the teachers, Amelia, and me for 2½ hours. I took notes throughout. Their questions stimulated us to reflect on how we had changed, and the effect on us, the families, and children.

Wanting Change

Wendy had a long story. After 20 years as a preschool teacher, she discovered she wanted to change but didn't know how. She read the MELC's ad soliciting teacher applicants, but had no idea what she would see. The school today was so different from when she arrived and from where she had worked before. There, all the children sat at desks all day, not what she wanted. She recalled how, during her interview, I told her some of my dreams, things she had not heard before. The MELC was her first experience with inner-city children. She had survived changes in directors. She had been receptive to my reports after each trip to Reggio, and recalled sitting for hours, sometimes until 9 at night, to hear the ideas. She felt she was in the right place, that allowing children to make their own choices was giving them respect. Most schools do not give a choice. Over the last 2 years, she had seen the school just . . . at a loss for words, Wendy concluded, "It's just what I want!"

Vea expressed appreciation that Reggio was a good reference and could speak to Wendy's feelings. She was impressed at the connections with Amelia, that with Wendy's long experience something in Reggio could help her. Wendy's story reminded her of her own experience and aroused similar emotions.

Jennifer recalled how much she had changed by recounting what she felt on Amelia's first morning—in a word, desperate. Amelia asked each teacher what she would be doing that day. Jennifer was so unsure of her role that a simple question triggered an outpouring of emotion. Uncertain and confused, Jennifer had withdrawn, running down the hall crying, frustrated, alone. She did not know what she should be doing and was embarrassed in front of Amelia. Now, at the end of Amelia's residency, everything was different, the purpose of what they were doing was so clear. Now if she cried it was with a sense of being overwhelmed by the positive changes she felt, as a person, in her life, in everything she did.

Slowing the Pace

Sonya recalled Amelia's observation that everything was fast-moving. In the Dining Room, children were eating lunch, shoveling in the food! Sonya described Amelia's reaction—her hand on her chin, an expression on her face that made Sonya think, "Oh! We're going to get it today at our staff meeting." She recalled Amelia's saying, "Okay, guys. I don't understand. Why was everybody eating so fast?"

We had never really thought about it, but Amelia had. She had timed it— 12 minutes! Sonya said, "Impossible!" Amelia followed the children to the bathroom, saw the amount of movement—zip, zip, zip—and asked: Why? Sonya explained they had to be out because the next group was coming. Amelia responded: "Okay, we need to slow everything down. We're going to start with the Dining Room. I want the teachers to sit at the table and have conversations with the children. Have everyone stay until everyone is finished."

Sonya noted how much things changed as a result, that lunch could last an hour, and the children had social exchanges. When Vea asked how the children responded, the teachers chorused: "They loved it!" The teachers described how they changed the routine, after lunch bringing everyone from the Dining Room to the Big Room and from there, three or four at a time, to the bathroom and then to the Nap Room.

Jennifer remembered that they added things to the Dining Room. The teachers bought place mats and flowers. Families sent utensils and other items from home. Vea acknowledged that when you don't merely use, but live in, a space, it is more like home and you take pleasure in it. Amelia helped us use the Dining Room as a place to live, not just a place to make it through mealtimes. When I recalled that the Dining Room had been hard and stark, but became soft and beautiful, Vea said the difference can result from defining a room's function.

Carlina asked if it was easy for us to change pace, how we felt, whether our relationships changed. Jennifer responded that three people in her life had asked her to slow down, her father, a woman with whom she'd camped, and now Amelia. She recalled that, during the dinosaur project, Amelia asked her to slow down and take very careful notes. She remembered her shock in reading those notes—how much she pushed Alonzo, how she rushed herself and him to make decisions when neither understood what had happened. "Why did I give him another piece of paper?" she recalled thinking. She disliked what she had done. Alonzo was drawing the tail, but she identified the problem, not giving him a chance to see the problem for himself. In that incident she began to understand how to help him, how they should work together, how she should let him go, how important it was not to jump at solutions too quickly.

Vea sympathized with her, saying that adults have a different concept of time and pacing than a child. She noted that when one is observed, it helps one observe oneself and it is the same for children. The adult gives the child more eyes with which to look at himself. Vea said that Amelia's strategy to observe the school for an initial period of 10 days was optimal. It prepared us to observe beyond her observation.

Deborah recalled how scared she was when she started as classroom manager (see Chapter 7), a role that required her to oversee all the children neither engaged in a project nor working with another teacher. She didn't understand what to do, and didn't want to do anything bad. Initially, she felt the atmosphere was restless with lots of movement, children taking something, barely using it, and quickly returning it to the shelf. Then Amelia stepped in, asking Wendy to show Deborah how to manage the classroom. Wendy helped her slow the pace by talking with the children about what they were choosing. Before that, children just went from thing to thing. Wendy told her to ask children what area they wanted to work in. As a result they slowed down, became engaged for longer times, and she came to know them better. She no longer had any problems.

Carlina asked what helped Jennifer feel more comfortable working with the children. Without hesitating, Jennifer said having a separate Dining Room instead of using the Studio for breakfast and lunch enabled the Studio to be her place; she didn't have to rush the children out while they were still socializing, or rush Studio activities to make way for a meal. As a result, she began to understand that when children came in, it was a time not to do something or get through one activity in order to start another, but rather to have an experience, to be with children as people, to approach each activity with the children with the same attitude she approached one of her own pieces of art. She ceased feeling rushed and became able to engage in lengthy experiences.

Engaging in Conversations

When Carlina asked Genet what made her comfortable, she replied it was learning she was not there to tell the children what to do but to listen to them, to help when they needed help, not to teach like a teacher. She felt better knowing the children had something to offer to her, that she did not have to be the one to offer everything. And she had realized this in her first conversation. Beforehand, she had not known what to do and was extremely anxious: What was she supposed to tell the children? She asked the other teachers how to have a conversation. They actually devoted a meeting to developing a list of questions, which she wrote down. At the first question the children took over! That's when she knew her role was to listen, to take notes, to be there to help if they needed.

Sonya explained how she had broadened her understanding of the value of conversation and how to hold conversations. The teachers hung utensils from home in the Dining Room, but Amelia noted that to give the utensils meaning there needed to be a panel with children's comments. However, the teachers didn't know how to elicit such comments—what questions to ask, what to say, when to stop, whether to cut the children off. Amelia told them to brainstorm questions as a staff, making a list. This made Sonya a little more comfortable, but she was still worried because the conversation would have to flow from the children's responses, not follow a list of questions. The need for specific information—a connection between the utensils and the children's comments—helped her realize how to focus a conversation and keep the children on track.

Wendy explained what had helped her—knowing you can go in, have the conversation, and stay as long as the children's interest is there. If you prepared 10 questions, you had time to wait for the answers to each, to pursue the conversation, and really listen.

Sonya explained that a breakthrough in understanding the importance of conversation occurred when the teachers started working on projects. At first, they did not really understand what they were doing. At the morning full-group meeting they discussed what they, the teachers, were going to do, but did not invite the children to share what was going on with them. In an "aha!" moment she realized that the teachers should use this meeting to converse with the children about what everyone would be doing that morning or had done recently.

Becoming Collaborators

Carlina asked if working as a group made the teachers feel more secure or made things more difficult. Wendy was emphatic: "More secure!" Formerly, not everyone offered opinions. Now everyone had a voice, one person no longer dominating meetings. Wendy explained how Amelia said, "What do you think about this, Deborah? What do you think about this, Wendy?" It helped them listen to everyone's opinion. Jennifer agreed, but added that it hadn't been easy and still wasn't. It meant putting herself out there, her insecurities, fears. She found it hard to state an opinion, especially if she disagreed. They had, however, improved at working as a group and trying to share opinions. When Amelia asked if they felt they were a group now, Jennifer and Wendy answered emphatically: "Yes! Yes!"

I recounted how I had sent memos, addressing them to Sonya and Wendy, co-head teachers. One day the staff asked to meet with me, all five coming to my office. I was worried! Were they all going to resign? Had something terrible happened? But it was the memos. First I assumed it was the content or tone, and was confused. Why would memos occasion such a momentous meeting? They had never come to my office en masse before. They said, "We only meet as a group. Don't send memos to Sonya and Wendy. Send memos to us all!" I was so relieved. They were asking for something so easy to do, which simply had not occurred to me. Yet it represented something enormously important—their collaborative spirit.

Responsive Families

When Carlina asked about families, Wendy responded that everyone pitched in, we had beautiful families, the best, that this year had been great! Genet echoed, adding that families surprised us every day with things they would never have done before. She exclaimed, "This year we ask once!" She explained that our increased communication with families showed them we respected them and their children. And they were proud, not only of their children but of the school.

Carlina asked how we started, if we could recall the moment when we realized families would respond. For Genet, it was families' excitement about the trip to the pumpkin patch. So many families came; before the trip the families were more excited than the children. Parents didn't just come themselves, but brought other family members. They understood the importance of family. "The turnout!" Genet exclaimed. "That's when I understood."

For Wendy, it started with the communication, sharing with families, getting them involved in what we were doing—in projects, collecting letters, numbers. Parents would comment, "My child wants to collect leaves to take to school." For Sonya, it started with the families' responses to questionnaires about their concerns. She realized how important the school had become when she saw responses like, "Will we have a first grade here? When are you going to open one?"

Expressing Feelings

When Carlina asked Amelia to describe her feelings, she said she felt at home here, she had found a school, people who could cooperate, who were available, who provided support and energy, who could understand her, her language, her context. She had a feeling of well-being, of enormous respect for these human beings. She felt the trust and confidence were unique. When people said to the staff, "You are lucky because you found Amelia," she responded, "I am lucky because I found them!"

Carlina asked about my feelings. I was amazed at the changes. Amelia appreciated the teachers' availability; I knew it was hard to be open, to expose one's flaws to a group, not to be defensive. Milestones for me were the teachers' not resigning after the many changes in director; their persevering when I returned from Reggio with only one answer to their many questions. Then Amelia agreed to a residency. Now I walked through the school and was in awe: The teachers had accomplished so much.

Appreciating Our Accomplishments

Vea recounted that participants in the MELC Day that was in session when she and Carlina arrived told them stories about problems in U.S. education, especially of difficulties in involving families. After 20 years in a school, she could read the environment. What she saw—huge amounts of work, intelligent thoughts, true respect for children—really moved her, completely. She had not expected anything like this. She was not making an official statement, but wanted to share her feelings as a person. She had heard what we said about our own feelings and wanted to thank and congratulate us.

Vea asked if the staff would be concerned if Amelia left, if they thought they could continue. Wendy explained that Amelia had been there for only 23 of their 36 weeks, that they worked just as hard when Amelia was away. "*Hard!*" Wendy repeated. Jennifer commented that, when she visited Reggio, she was struck that she understood, that she could read their environment. That meant, hopefully, Amelia had not just shown them *what* to do but *how* to do it. If they continued observing, analyzing themselves and the children, they could succeed. "Yes," Vea acknowledged. She believed we could.

What we had done, Vea said, was a reflection of the teachers' work, Ann's, and Amelia's. We had shown people in Reggio that they could be optimistic about schools elsewhere. They saw the MELC as a poster of the possibilities outside the context of Reggio, an example of what can happen when people with the same thoughts work together. She could not predict the future, but hoped we would continue. The school would need someone persistent like Ann, like Amelia, like these teachers. Persistence was important everywhere in the United States. She strongly believed that, were Malaguzzi here, he would recognize the effort and appreciate the work a lot. She added that it was not so easy now, either here or in Reggio. At the time, I did not catch the implicit warning. Looking back, her words appeared ominous.

Carlina said this was her personal opinion too; she agreed completely with Vea. She was less surprised because she was here last year. Many things had changed, some completely. Last year she saw possibility, now reality. She had known Amelia many years but what she saw here was completely new. It was important that, when she talked with us, the words were familiar, as if we were talking the same language. She was particularly struck by the relationship between adults and children.

Carlina found it extraordinary to think that it happened in one year, even sooner because the past is in the present. She felt it was good for us all, in Reggio, in the United States. She had not thought they would find a situation that shows what it means to really apply the Reggio approach. "As you know," she said, "it is not simple." She concluded we could be proud, but not relax. We had a new responsibility. Many others were looking at us. She and Vea would report to Reggio Children: They would recommend this as a situation they could look at with lots of attention and hope.

Carlina cautioned that, as they learned in Reggio, this was an arrival, not the end. There is always a new mountain from which to see the vista. Most important to Carlina was what MELC Day participants had told her: "It is unbelievable what we saw in that school."

CHAPTER 11

Epilogue

If the community fails to support the desires and standards of school people, the educators are destined to fail.

Howard Gardner

For anyone interested in changing schools, the MELC's closing is as instructive as its success. If there were any one cause, it would be funding. But it could have been changes in leadership; or the nature of systems; or the system of one particular organization. The school was intimately tied to the atmosphere then pervading Washington. It was also a casualty of the prevalent attitudes in our culture toward young children.

A LEADER LEAVES

In 1989 Bennis said that leaders "persist because they are unwilling to settle for anything less than the best. [Their] passion, energy, and focus beget passion, energy, and focus in their workers" (p. 109). A decade later he (with Biederman, 1997) added: "They are curators, whose job is not to make, but to choose . . . [and who are] confident enough to recruit people better than themselves. They revel in the talent of others" (pp. 200–201).

Bennis could have been describing my role. First I realized that preschools could be different, then identified ones that were, and adapted their practices. Gardner (1995) calls such actions "considerable agency" and says they come about because of "authoritative position and . . . powers of persuasion" (p. 295).

For 20 years I had "considerable agency" at The National Learning Center. Of all our programs, I was most passionate about the MELC. But after December 1994 my responsibilities as president and executive director ended. At age 55 and divorced many years, I left Washington to marry Robert Benham and move to Memphis, Tennessee. However, Reggio's accreditation required me to remain as director of the Model Early Learning Center through June 1995. From a thousand miles away, I tried to stay involved by paper and telephone, read memos between the teachers and the new executive director, and sensed the teachers' increasing distress at changes happening throughout the organization, especially their deepening concern that the MELC was not valued among TNLC's programs. Returning periodically to lead MELC Days, I listened to the teachers—with sympathy and dismay. I laid out a fund-raising strategy. But I was no longer the leader.

FUNDING PROBLEMS

When I left, Washington was entering a period of financial chaos that impacted many public and private organizations. Because the MELC's funding came from the U.S. Congress, the school was dependent on Congressmen's attitudes toward Washington's low-income residents. It was also dependent on its contractual relationship with the D.C. Public Schools, which was being rent simultaneously by the city's problems and by its own. In addition to external sources, the school depended on The National Learning Center's board, which considered the museum's funding paramount to the MELC's. These three factors imperiled the school financially.

Congressional Contact Lost

Political power emanating from the highest government echelons permeates many facets of Washington. The city, as well as many nongovernment organizations in the metropolitan area, depend on Congressional funding, where relationships have long histories and can mean life or death for a program. Having a president's wife interested in your program or a cabinet member's wife on the board, having a member of Congress or someone with access to a congressional committee support an initiative, can determine whether a program survives. Unlike the museum, which had diverse funding, after an initial surge of private funds, the MELC relied almost solely on its Congressional line item. In 1995 these political realities hit the MELC, the aftermath of an earlier occurrence.

Two years before, on May 27, 1993, *The Washington Post* had reported: "The District collectively gasped, then slumped in anguish with the announcement that D.C. Council Chairman John A. Wilson was dead" (p. J1). An editorial 6 weeks later began:

> The void left by the death of John Wilson has proved to be enormous and is only now beginning to be fully understood as his skills and contributions over the years keep on coming to light. Who among the seven candidates seeking the chairmanship has [his] . . . political knowledge, candor, courage and clout? ("Lineup for Council chairman," 1993, p. C6)

The ramifications of Wilson's death would reverberate widely and be felt for years. They hit the MELC hard.

John had served on TNLC's board for 17 years—from the time of his first political foray in the 1970s as a school board member, through various political positions, to his council chairmanship in the 1990s. John was a dedicated public servant, ferociously bright, attractive, especially fast with numbers, in turn charismatic, cranky, outspoken. When you dealt with John, you always knew where he stood. Everyone trusted him. Members and staff of the District Committee believed that John understood the city's finances, their area of concern; many on the Hill believed he was the only person who understood them. They also trusted that he could control spending. Through his elections to increasingly higher positions, John remained TNLC's staunch supporter. With John gone, no one could satisfy Congress that Washington's finances were under control. The impact was felt by huge organizations like the D.C. government and by small organizations like The National Learning Center.

The local political climate was highly charged after John's death, many candidates vying for his council seat. The situation was complicated by funding problems so severe that Congress threatened to revoke the city's charter. The city was in free fall, politically and financially. Had John lived, he singlehandedly could have found a place in the city's massive budget for the MELC's small allotment. His successor had no interest in the MELC.

Partnership with Contractor Deteriorated

The D.C. Public Schools was the Congressionally authorized recipient of the federal funds that supported the MELC and thereby our contractor. In 1995 the public school system was in turmoil. Its operations had been reviewed by a high-powered external management group that alleged every conceivable problem—corruption, cronyism, incompetence. Excerpts from the study surfaced for weeks in the *Washington Post*, causing a furor that left the school system reeling.

The superintendent, Dr. Franklin Smith, faced a plight typical of big-city superintendents: For reasons not of his making, his administration was on the way out along with his programs and people, among them Maurice Sykes, who oversaw the MELC's contract. Under Dr. Smith, Sykes's position as Head of Early Childhood had expanded when *early* was redefined as continuing through second grade; then Sykes was made head of Elementary Education, and eventually deputy superintendent.

Sykes, an inspired administrator, is a nationally recognized early childhood educator. An innovator within a major public school system, Sykes had launched a bold endeavor, the Center for Systemic Educational Change, and had established Cadre Teachers, early childhood educators who, recognized for their excellence, would undertake special initiatives—lectures, enrichment, trial programs—and share what they learned throughout the system. Angered by years of neglect under other administrators, Sykes had big plans to inspire teachers, and had actually placed orders to fully equip all kindergartens. Working closely with Maurice, TNLC had contracted in 1994 to acquaint the Cadre Teachers with the Reggio Approach.

At TNLC we felt the impact of the public school system's gathering storm. At the beginning of school year 1994–95 it took a huge effort to generate our contracts. Even when signed, it required enormous politicking to generate the payments stipulated in the contracts. I enlisted everyone I knew on Capitol Hill, on the District Board of Education, and throughout the school system's administration. We did not suspect at the time that Smith's and Sykes's tenures were ending. Had we foreseen the resulting problems, we might have tried to establish the MELC as an independent entity, found a die-hard director, implored a funder to endow it, or put it under one of Washington's two Head Start administrations. Smith's and Sykes's departures left a leadership vacuum: No one in D.C. Public Schools had the authority to support the MELC, or the daring to defend it.

Board Attention Attenuated

Washington's highly charged political milieu had a peculiar effect on leadership in not-for-profit organizations. Civic pride is different in Washington, where the federal government funds and runs some of the most prestigious institutions, which elsewhere private boards fund and run. When leading local citizens run such institutions, they become stakeholders, taking responsibility for their town's quality of life. In Washington many of the most prominent trustees are political appointments controlled by the President of the United States, national personalities who have no stake in the city's well-being. Washington trustees are sometimes more committed to who is on a board than to an organization's mission. New and still fragile with a single source of funding, the MELC's survival depended on its leaders' commitment. It was not that those with ultimate authority for the MELC thought anything was wrong with the school. More likely, with the city feeling as if it might collapse, TNLC leaders were otherwise occupied. With its board's and executive director's fund-raising efforts focused elsewhere, no one sought funds for the MELC.

A MATTER OF SYSTEMS

Exceptional innovators, Maria Montessori and Loris Malaguzzi each espoused a philosophy and made it the basis for complex, robust school systems, generally drawing passionately committed families or significant government support. These systems resonated with the best features of the Italian culture, and in the century when they spread worldwide, Montessori schools resonated with numerous other cultures as the Reggio Approach does today. But unlike America's suburban Montessori schools, the MELC's parents were not primed through their own experience or the school's urging to be advocates. And unlike the schools in Reggio, the MELC never became part of a complex system that was integrally tied to its community's social, economic, and political life.

Administrators attempting systemic change must encourage both the immediate and broader communities to share values, and must imbue their entire system—administration, funding, parents, community—with theories that are consistent with practice. If parents' beliefs are at odds with a school's, if politicians and the public hold different values, the change will not last. The macroissues of community and system and the microissue of classroom practices, while different, are equally important.

The Reggio schools exemplify a system in which the macro- and microissues are well balanced, there is no disabling bureaucracy, and the entire system has strong theoretical underpinnings. The schools serve a large percentage of their city's young children. Daily activities are capable of change. The system nurtures continuity. These schools have endured over time, and their approach is consistent across all 32 schools. The system's integrity elicits teachers' trust; the invigorating conditions evoke their passion; that passion has drawn the world's attention.

The bureaucratic problems that often beset new initiatives in public or private schools had not impacted the MELC. Sheltered by Sykes's belief in what we were attempting and by my nurturing, the school had the freedom to keep on trying—almost to sink at first, to flounder for 2 years, but to right itself, and finally to accomplish something significant. However, the autonomy essential for its establishment became a contributing factor in its downfall.

We do not understand enough about individuals or complex systems to predict how much stress they can tolerate before the individual loses motivation or the system collapses. Nor do we understand enough about how to build and maintain the kinds of structures that support complexity. The MELC flourished in a time and place with a critical mass of supportive circumstances. It rested on the shared vision of myself and Sykes and on my political dance for congressional funding—granted for 9 years, through the (first) Bush and into the Clinton administrations, but never for more than 12 months at a time. But, in our culture, people come and go—even as Sykes left the D.C. Public Schools after 22 years and I left TNLC after 20. The MELC had depended on our mutual admiration. Outside his purview in the public school system and mine at TNLC, the MELC was not woven into an institution.

ORGANIZATIONAL CHANGES

The National Learning Center and its programs emerged several years after the Capital Children's Museum had been established, and the museum remained the more prominent entity locally. For many of its trustees, the museum was the organization's raison d'être and the cause for their board membership. That commitment and the shifting mind-set among upper-level staff after I left had grave consequences for the MELC.

Triage

Trustee Frances Humphrey Howard, long-time TNLC board member and sister of the late vice president, wrote to me in March 1995: "None of us who are board members know what the fate of . . . [TNLC] will be. We only know that . . . funding is increasingly difficult, particularly since the city is going to go through very hard times with the new Congress." Desperate for funding in an increasingly hostile climate, board members chose among TNLC's entities: Teacher education programs would end when the contracts supporting them expired. Options School's appropriation provided significant indirect costs and excellent cash flow; thus they would not close it. But the MELC's appropriation covered only direct costs. So they put their effort into funding the museum, leaving the MELC with a weakening funding source and without the leadership either to secure it or to find other sources.

The board was not fully mindful of the MELC's import beyond TNLC. The museum, locally a precious resource, was one of an increasing number of similar institutions nationally. Likewise, Options School was one of an increasing number of small programs to serve school dropouts. While both were exemplary, programs elsewhere could serve as models. But, in letting the MELC close, the board created a vacuum: At the time, there were few preschools in the United States where early educators could see the Reggio Approach.

A Managerial Perspective

Mission drives nonprofit organizations: they exist to stage inspiring performances, display acclaimed art, offer advanced medical treatment, develop students' highest capacities. Leaders in nonprofits are mission driven, innovative,
and entrepreneurial. These traits create inherent tension between leader and
manager. In contrast to leaders, managers "never [look] beyond the bottom line,
[are] more concerned with cutting costs than improving the product, eschew innovation and, above all, rank careful management over creative entrepreneur-
ship" (Bennis, 1989, p. 83). After I left, each new executive director of TNLC was
a careful manager, and worked under a board that became deeply involved in
management. As their beliefs, personalities, and actions took hold, many issues
surfaced that, from 1995 on, undermined the MELC teachers' motivation, changed
their relationship with the executive director, and ultimately contributed to the
school's closing.

During my first month in Memphis, I sent a memo to the board and to the
new executive director:

> *Jeopardy of the Model Early Learning Center*:
> The teachers have been told that there is no guarantee they will be
> paid during the remainder of the current school year . . . and they
> have no date by which they will be told if they will be hired next
> year. Under these conditions, they are all making alternate work
> plans. (February 1995)

This contrasted markedly with the Reggio educators who constantly sent
memos, letters, and exchanges of gifts. In accrediting us, Reggio Children committed to support of 33 schools—32 in their town plus ours in Washington. The teachers
relied on this support. For example, on February 9, 1995, Eletta Bertani, president
of Reggio Children, wrote:

> To the teachers, the parents, the children: After a public evening
> about your school, with . . . the mayor and other local authorities,
> where Amelia Gambetti has presented, with many slides and a
> video, your experience of the last 2 years . . . we feel the need to
> express to all of you, . . . a school we consider "sister" of the Reggio
> schools, our feelings. . . . Even [though] the distance between
> Reggio and Washington is huge, dear friends, we feel that every-
> thing you have been doing is very close to our ideas and feelings
> . . . and we send you the feelings of friendship and solidarity.

In April 1995 the teachers had a tense meeting with the executive director
over the MELC's future. When they asked forthrightly if he wanted them to stay,
he replied that they were all fine teachers, but he knew many fine teachers. The
teachers interpreted the answer to mean that they were expendable.

In trying to keep the MELC afloat financially, the executive director proposed
that a percentage of MELC families pay tuition. Knowing this would force many
withdrawals, the teachers were greatly disturbed. But the uppermost threat was

the proposal to change the MELC to a laboratory school for unidentified researchers. Perhaps the executive director thought a lab school would attract research funding. The teachers, however, felt they would be, in their word, violated. To them, children's needs, not researchers', were paramount. The executive director had surely not intended to be high-handed, but it seemed so to the teachers. They had recently remade themselves into a close-knit, trusting collaborative that engaged in lengthy discussions about any changes, no matter how small. It seemed like hubris for a new executive, unfamiliar with the school, to propose so major a change, and eliminated any vestige of their trust in him.

A Crack in a Relationship

With uncertainty swirling in The National Learning Center, the Reggio leadership questioned whether to renew accreditation. A May 1, 1995, memo to the MELC teachers from the executive director said accreditation would not drive his decisions in regard to the school's programs and policies. The teachers' interpretation of his statement was that the relationship with Reggio, their lifeblood, mattered little to him. His apparent dismissal of accreditation, which had been hard won and reflected a standard of excellence, lost the teachers' respect.

By spring 1996 a further distressing change was the increased frequency of MELC Days. TNLC charged each attendee $235, and with few direct expenses and many participants, the program was valuable financially. How many MELC Days to offer became a contentious issue. Jennifer resigned in January 1997, not finishing the school year, in part because she felt the increased number was taking the teachers away from the children too often.

It is difficult to attend to work when an organization's future is in question. By school year 1996–97 the teachers were disheartened, not knowing if they would have jobs, feeling that the school—their passion—was not valued, hanging on primarily because of their commitment to the children and families.

REGGIO CONNECTION SEVERED

Amelia had first visited the MELC in school year 1992–93; she had been in residence a substantial part of the following year, and had spent several weeks in the MELC in fall and spring of school year 1994–95. Subsequently, she maintained close contact with the MELC teachers. Attitudes of the MELC's leaders, its funding perils, and the teachers' discomfort were felt more keenly in Reggio than in Washington.

The MELC lost its accreditation in spring 1997. An open letter from Reggio Children (1997) reported:

> No connections or basis for continuing the collaboration exist. . . . The repeated changes in leadership and the changes that have occurred this school year [1996–97] in the structure, schedule, staff ratio, and clientele have seriously jeopardized the relationship that had lasted for several years. . . . However . . . the experience that took place from September 1993 to December 1996 . . . has a value that nothing will ever damage or diminish.

The brief article stated that Reggio Children's connection with the MELC had been severed. The MELC closed in June 1997. As word spread, the growing number of educators who knew of the MELC or had visited collectively gasped. It was unthinkable that the school could close.

SO, WHAT HAPPENED?

The MELC was ultimately undone by many factors: When I moved away from Washington, the top executives of the DCPS, who were the MELC's contracting officers, came under fire at the same time as the city entered a period of near financial collapse; the MELC lost both its leadership and its funding simultaneously. Concurrently, unfavorable local situations—the death of a powerful city council chairman who had supported the MELC and a huge budget fiasco in the U.S. Congress, the source of the MELC's finances—coincided with a period when national attitudes toward the kind of values represented in the MELC were hardening. The MELC emphasized individual growth and lateral thinking at a time of pressure for increased testing. Testing forced children to be measured against a monolithic standard and forced teachers to focus on increasingly lock-step thinking, focuses that were inimical to the MELC. Finally, the MELC's classroom practices were not woven into a system of community and administrative support, both of which are essential for a school to survive, much less to flourish. Taken together, this complex of circumstances was too much for the MELC's still incipient structure.

Loss of Leadership and Funding

At the end of December 1994 I left; soon after, top administrators left the D.C. Public Schools, and shortly before, John Wilson, a major supporter, had died. The city itself was in dire financial difficulty, causing funding problems. In fall 1994 the MELC's contract with the D.C. Public Schools was delayed, caught up in Congress's withholding the city's entire appropriation. In subsequent years it was questioned, cut, then eliminated. Although we could not see it, as I left Washington the end of the TNLC/DCPS partnership, which was the MELC's lifeline, was beginning.

Washington anomalies exacerbated the problems. From the mighty Kennedy Center and National Symphony to Capital Children's Museum, executive directors in Washington court Congress members for funding, even without an elected Congressman as advocate. After my departure no one at TNLC did, so the MELC lost its relationship on the Hill. With that loss went the school's entire funding base.

Lack of Support for Young Children

Values surrounding childhood—not those espoused but those actually practiced—impacted the school. In the small city of Reggio Emilia the high quality of its increasingly famous preschools is cause for celebration. In our large city the MELC was scarcely noticed. Had it been, it might have been viewed with suspicion, a reception our culture sometimes gives to anything too far from the middle of the road, whether excellent or deplorable. Moreover, our culture's response to emerging research on young children has been, by and large, to productize child-hood, not to professionalize caregiving. "Cosmetologists must attend as much as 2,000 hours of training before getting a license, but thirty states allow teachers in child care centers to work with children without any training in early childhood development" (Children's Defense Fund, 2002, page 55).

Child advocate Marian Wright Edelman says:

> As we face . . . a new millennium, the overarching challenge for America is to rebuild a sense of community and hope and civility and caring and safety . . . and to give back to all of our children their sense of security and their ability to dream about and work toward a future that is attainable and hope-ful. (Edelman, 1995, p. xxviii)

At no time in its existence did sociocultural influences impinge more strongly on the MELC than in the last 2 years.

Lack of an Integrated System

The history of American education reflects numerous efforts to change and many successful projects. Few continue; but the question persists: Why are change efforts not sustained? I believe they disappear because they cannot be translated from a single successful instance—a great teacher or single fine school—to a system of education that can serve a critical mass of children. Or they stray too far from the cultural norm. Or the population they are intended to serve lacks the resources to effect support. Were I starting today, I would address community and system be-fore working on classroom practices in order to assure a school's exis-tence. Howard Gardner, reflecting on the MELC's closing and other such efforts, said, "Like meteors, they go up high, then crash. There are two separate phenomena, the difficulty of taking an example from one place and replicating it elsewhere and the disappearance of the charismatic leader" (Personal Communication, September 2002).

The teachers were doing a superhuman job, spending 60 hours or more each week with the children or together in meetings. The reward was the creative process, not the salary. In Csikszentmihalyi's words, they were in "flow state." But motiva-tion is fragile, especially for teachers who, like artists, work to excess, have passionate feelings, and do the untried. Changes in leadership ultimately imposed constraints on the teachers, and they in turn lost respect for their leaders. Freedom and autonomy enhance motivation; constraints, whether real or perceived, kill it. Given the volatil-ity in so many areas, it is amazing that the teachers retained any motivation.

For several years circumstances surrounding the school had been motivat-ing: The teachers had the freedom to pursue a vision, the funding for what they needed, nurturing in support of their effort, and accolades from their leaders, from visitors, and the press. A powerful limelight shone on them. From 1995 on, chang-ing circumstances diminished their freedom, eliminated the funding, and ended the nurturing. Visitors and the press still came, so for a while they remained in the limelight. But limelight alone could not sustain the school.

Any single factor—Washington's imploding finances, the public schools' collapsing administration, changes at TNLC, my emphasis on practice over struc-ture, a culture of childhood that is more noise than nurture, the constraints the teachers felt—might not have hurt the school. Everything together was more than it could bear.

HOPEFUL SIGNS

> *The question was put to him what hope is; and his answer was, "The dream of a waking man."*
>
> Diogenes Laertius

Today, there is strong interest in the Reggio schools; inspired by them, many educators around the world, including in the United States, are trying to adapt their approach. There is an association of schools—the North American Reggio Education Association—that tries to assist the increasing numbers who want to learn about or hope to follow the Reggio educators. Reggio educators themselves recognized this need in the early 1990s and responded by establishing their own international organization, Reggio Children, to try to find ways to answer increasing calls from around the world for information, assistance, and inspiration.

Like anything new, and especially in education, what becomes mainstream takes time to root. We must remember that Reggio practices are strongly rooted in their culture. Moreover, these roots were laid over several decades so that today the schools and their culture are inextricably linked. In this regard as in so many others, the Reggio educators are on the leading edge. American educators who are inspired to try Reggio's approach have strong examples to follow; in fact, they have a new vision of what early education can be.

The efforts of American educators who are using Reggio practices are vitally important. Their work can provide examples for the culture at large of new avenues for young children's growth, of ways to establish collaborative endeavors to nurture children, and of what we all—anyone who cares about the next generation—must do by way of support. These educators are pioneers, overcoming pitfalls and forging solutions. Their attempts are creating markers to lead the way for others. Amelia Gambetti refers to it as an "evolution" and says there are some teachers whose efforts are important in raising the quality of their work (Personal Communication, March 2004).

As this movement spreads, and it surely will, what we accomplished in the Model Early Learning Center should be a harbinger for what is possible for schools everywhere. It proves that a strong program can help overcome constraints that the environment imposes on children. It shows that a staff of passionate, committed teachers can accomplish enormous feats. The growth of Reggio practices in American schools will happen, as any great change does, one effort at a time. One parent, one teacher, one school, or one community can be the impetus for the success of a new endeavor.

The fact that the MELC flourished is cause for optimism. Knowing that something can be done is a powerful spur for others' attempts. Ultimately, the purpose of this book is to provide a clear narrative about the Model Early Learning Center so that its story will inform and inspire anyone who tries to make possible schools a reality.

References

AFL-CIO. (2005). Facts about working women. Retrieved May 23, 2005, from AFL/ CIO.www.aflcio.org/issuespolitics/women/factsaboutworkingwomen.cfm

Ashton-Warner, S. (1963). *Teacher*. New York: Bantam.

Beer, S. (1974). Managing modern complexity (pp. 86–96). In H. VonFoerster (Ed.), *Cybernetics of cybernetics*. Urbana: University of Illinois.

Bennis, W. (1989). *Why leaders can't lead*. San Francisco: Jossey-Bass.

Bennis, W., & Biederman, P. W. (1997). *Organizing genius: The secrets of creative collaboration*. Reading MA: Addison-Wesley.

Campani, G., Fornaciari, I., & Forghieri, E. (1983). *Notebooks*. Municipality of Reggio Emilia: Department of Education, Infant and Toddler Centers and Kindergartens.

Caro, R. A. (1974). *The power broker*. New York: Vintage.

Children's Defense Fund. (2002). *Mini green book*. Washington, DC. Retrieved May 23, 2005, from http://www.childrensdefensefund.org/pdf/minigreenbook.pdf

Cool, S. J. (1996). Developmental neuro-optometry: The scientific basis for the functional approach to vision care behavioral optometry. Retrieved June 19, 2005, from http://www.babouse.org/cool.html

Csikszentmihalyi, M. (1990). *Motivation: Key to the kingdom*? Unpublished manuscript.

Csikszentmihalyi, M. (1993). *The evolving self*. New York: HarperCollins.

Dalaker, J. (2001). *Poverty in the United States: 2000*. U.S. Census Bureau. Retrieved June 12, 2005 from http://www.census.gov/prod/2001pubs/p60-214.pdf Table D. Percent of People in Poverty by State.

Damasio, A. (1994). *Descartes' error*. New York: HarperCollins.

De Cuevas, J. (1990, September-October). No, she holded them loosely. *Harvard Magazine, 93*(1), 65–66.

Diogenes (ca. 300 A.D.). *Lives of eminent philosophers* (R. D. Hicks, Trans., 1925). Cambridge: Harvard University Press. Aristotle v18, p. 461.

Edelman, M. W. (1995). *Guide my feet*. Boston: Beacon.

Edwards, C., Gandini, L., & Forman, G. (1998). *The hundred languages of children* (2nd ed.). Greenwich, CT: Ablex.

Feuerstein, R. (1988). *don't accept me as I am*. New York: Plenum.

Feuerstein, R., Klein, P., & Tannenbaum, A. (1991). *Mediated learning experience (MLE)*. London: Freund.

Forman, G., & Gandini, L. (Eds.). (1994). (Video). *An amusement park for birds*. Amherst, MA: Performanetics.

Gandini, L. (2001). Reggio Emilia: Experiencing life in an infant-toddler center. In L. Gandini & C. Edwards (Eds.), *Bambini: The Italian approach to infant/toddler care* (pp. 55–66). New York: Teachers College Press.

Gardner, H. (1983). *Frames of mind*. New York: BasicBooks.

Gardner, H. (1991). *The unschooled mind*. New York: BasicBooks.

Gardner, H. (1995). *Leading minds*. New York: BasicBooks.

Gardner, H. (2000). *The disciplined mind: Beyond facts and standardized tests, the K–12 education that every child deserves*. New York: Penguin.

Ghedini, P. (2001). Change in Italian national policy for children 0–3 years old and their families: Advocacy and responsibility. In L. Gandini & C. Edwards (Eds.), *Bambini: The Italian approach to infant/toddler care* (pp. 38–48). New York: Teachers College Press.

Gleick, J. (2003). *Isaac Newton.* New York: Pantheon.

Henderson, N. (1993, May 27). Working through the grief; city struggles to move on in aftermath of Wilson's death. *The Washington Post*, p. J1.

Lawrence, L. A. (1993, August 9). An Italian import for early education. *Christian Science Monitor*, p. 12.

Leonard, G. (1968). *Education and ecstasy.* New York: Dell.

Lewin, A. W. (1998). Bridge to another culture. In C. Edwards, L. Gandini, & G. Forman (Eds.), *The hundred languages of children* (2nd ed., pp. 335–357). Greenwich, CT: Ablex.

The lineup for council chairman [Editorial]. (1993, July 11). *The Washington Post*, p. C6.

Malaguzzi, L., & Filippini, T. (1991). *The very little ones of silent pictures.* Municipal Infant/ Toddler Centers of Reggio Emilia.

Montessori, M. (1962). *The discovery of the child* (M. A. Johnstone, Trans.). Adyar, India: Kalakshetra. (Original work published 1929)

Montessori, M. (1965). *The secret of childhood* (B. B. Carter, Trans.). Bombay: Orient Longmans. (Original work published 1936)

Municipality of Reggio Emilia, Department of Infant and Toddler Centers and Kindergartens. (1983). *Notebooks: The "diary" at the nursery school.*

Municipality of Reggio Emilia, Department of Infant and Toddler Centers and Kindergartens. (1990, November). *An historical outline data and information.*

Neufeld, M. (1994, May 21) Environment through the eyes of children: Youngest film makers focus on environment. *The Washington Times*, pp. B1, B6.

Ornstein, R., & Thompson, R. (1984). *The amazing brain.* Boston: Houghton Mifflin.

Perkins, D. (1992). *Smart schools.* New York: Free Press.

Project Zero/Reggio Children. (2001). *Making learning visible.* Cambridge, MA, and Reggio Emilia, Italy: Author

Rankin, Baji (1998). Curriculum development in Reggio Emilia: A long-term curriculum project about dinosaurs. In C. Edwards, L. Gandini, & G. Forman, *The hundred languages of children* (2nd ed., pp. 215–237). Greenwich, CT: Ablex.

Reggio Children. (1997, spring). An open letter from Reggio Children concerning the model early learning center. *Innovations*, Vol 5.1, p. 8.

Resnick, L. (1987). *Education and learning to think.* Washington, DC: National Academy Press.

Rinaldi, C. (1983). Introduction to Lara's story, *Notebooks.* Municipality of Reggio Emilia: Department of Education, Infant and Toddler Centers and Kindergartens.

Rinaldi, C. (1998). Projected curriculum constructed through documentation—*Progettazione.* In C. Edwards, L. Gandini, & G. Forman, *The hundred languages of children* (2nd ed., pp. 113–125). Greenwich, CT: Ablex.

Sacks, P. (1999). *Standardized minds.* Cambridge, MA: Perseus.

Spaggiari, S., Malaguzzi, L., & Dolci, M. (1990). Unpublished translation of *Everything has a shadow, except ants* (L. A. Lawrence, Trans.). Reggio Emilia, Italy: Municipality.

Stafford, W. (1978). *Writing the Australian crawl.* Ann Arbor: University of Michigan.

Thoreau, H. D. (1965). *Walden.* New York: Harper. (Original work published 1854)

Trejos, N. (2004, March 15). Time may be up for naps in pre-K class. *The Washington Post*, p. AO1.

U.S. National Commission on Excellence in Education. (1983). *A nation at risk: The imperative for educational reform.* Washington, DC: U.S. Department of Education.

Index

About the Author

Ann Lewin-Benham, a graduate of Bryn Mawr College, currently lives in Memphis, where she is consolidating 40 years' experience in school and museum education by writing. In 1988 she founded the Model Early Learning Center, a preschool for Head Start-eligible children in Washington, D.C. Also in Washington she founded, and for 20 years directed, the Capital Children's Museum—a large hands-on museum that was also a workshop for innovations in early childhood education, an after-school care provider for its inner-city neighborhood, and partner with Apple Computer and many other funders in groundbreaking programs. During that time she also founded Options School for teenagers chronically absent from school. In prior years she was a cofounder of Parkmont Junior High, an experimental school without walls. Trained as a Montessori teacher, she taught in one of the Washington area's first Montessori schools and later established Montessori classes in the Arlington County Public Schools.